The Complete Gnostic Gospels & Apocalypses

Ancient Rejected Christian Texts Questioning Orthodoxy—From Thomas to the Apocalypse of Peter

A Modern Translation

Adapted for the Contemporary Reader

Various Gnostic Writers

Translated by Tim Zengerink

Table of Contents

Preface - Message to the Reader

What If You Could Help Rebuild the Greatest Library in Human History?

Thousands of years ago, the Library of Alexandria stood as the crown jewel of human achievement — a sanctuary where the collected wisdom of every known civilization was gathered, preserved, and shared freely.

And then, it was lost.

Through fire, conquest, and the slow erosion of time, humanity lost not just books — but ideas, dreams, discoveries, and stories that could have changed the world forever.

Today, the Library of Alexandria lives again — and you are invited to be a part of its restoration.

Our mission is simple yet profound:

To rebuild the greatest library the world has ever known, and to translate all timeless works into every language and dialect, so that no seeker of knowledge is ever left behind again.

By joining our movement to rebuild the modern Library of Alexandria, you become part of an unprecedented mission:

- **Unlimited Access to the Greatest Audiobooks & eBooks Ever Written:**

    Instantly explore thousands of legendary works—Plato, Shakespeare, Jane Austen, Leo Tolstoy, and countless more. All instantly available to read or listen, placing a complete literary universe at your fingertips.

- **Beautiful Paperback & Deluxe Editions at Printing Cost**

  Own any title as an elegant paperback, deluxe hardcover, or stunning collectible boxset—offered to you at true printing cost, delivered straight to your door. Build your personal Library of Alexandria, crafted for beauty, built for durability, and worthy of proud display.

- **Fresh Translations for Modern Readers—in Every Language & Dialect**

  Enjoy timeless masterpieces reimagined in clear, contemporary language—no more outdated phrases or obscure references. Alongside the original versions, we're tirelessly translating these classics into every language and dialect imaginable, ensuring accessibility and understanding across cultures and generations.

- **Join a Global Renaissance of Literature & Knowledge**

  You directly support expanding our library, publishing deluxe editions at true cost, translating works into all global languages, and bringing humanity's greatest stories to people everywhere. By joining today, you're not just preserving a legacy of masterpieces; you set in motion a powerful wave of literary accessibility.

Become a Torchbearer of Knowledge.

Join us for free now at **LibraryofAlexandria.com**

Together, we will ensure that the light of human wisdom never fades again.

With gratitude and a shared love of knowledge,
The Modern Library of Alexandria Team

Visit:

www.libraryofalexandria.com

Or scan the code below:

Introduction

A Hidden Heritage:
The Lost Voice of Early Christian Mysticism

In the ancient world, the question of truth was not a settled matter. While mainstream Christianity gradually coalesced around creeds, bishops, and canonized texts, many other voices continued to echo in the spiritual corridors of the early Church—voices that were passionate, provocative, and profoundly different. These were the voices of the Gnostics.

Gnosticism is not a single school of belief, but rather a broad and fluid tradition marked by its central emphasis on "gnosis"—a Greek word meaning knowledge. But this was no ordinary knowledge. It was hidden, sacred, intuitive, and salvific. To the Gnostic, salvation came not through dogma, external rituals, or blind obedience to authority, but through inner awakening—an experiential recognition of the divine spark within each soul.

The Complete Gnostic Gospels & Apocalypses brings together many of the most important and revealing writings from this ancient spiritual stream. These include well-known texts such as the Gospel of Thomas and Gospel of Mary, as well as lesser-known but equally profound works like Zostrianos, Marsanes, and the Apocalypse of Peter. These documents challenge orthodox assumptions, present alternative accounts of Jesus' mission, and offer an expansive cosmology that redefines the soul's relationship to the cosmos.

These writings were not simply forgotten—they were condemned, hidden, and in many cases destroyed. Yet they survived, buried in desert jars, copied in obscure monasteries, and rediscovered in places like Nag Hammadi in 1945. Now, in a time once again marked by spiritual searching and skepticism of institutional authority, these texts speak with fresh relevance. They invite us to reconsider what Christianity once was—and what it might yet become.

The Gnostic Vision:
Light in the Darkness

At the heart of Gnostic cosmology is the idea that the visible world is not the ultimate reality. According to many of these texts, the physical universe is not God's perfect creation, but rather the flawed handiwork of a lower divine being—the Demiurge—often identified with the Old Testament Creator. This being, along with his servants known as archons, obscures the true, invisible realm of the highest God—the Pleroma, or fullness.

In this cosmic drama, human beings are seen as divine souls trapped in material bodies. Our forgetfulness, pain, and mortality are not part of the original divine intention, but symptoms of our estrangement from the source. The role of the Savior—who is often identified with Jesus, though in radically reimagined form—is not merely to die as a sacrifice for sins, but to awaken the divine memory within us. Jesus becomes a revealer, a guide, a transmitter of liberating truth.

Texts like the Gospel of Thomas emphasize the immediacy of this inner revelation: "The kingdom is inside you, and it is outside you." The Gospel of Mary presents Mary Magdalene not as a repentant sinner, but as a teacher, mystic, and intimate confidante of the risen Christ—challenging patriarchal hierarchies and reasserting the spiritual equality of all seekers.

The Gospel of Judas reframes Judas not as a traitor, but as the only disciple who truly understood Jesus' plan—a stunning reversal of traditional roles meant to highlight the illusory nature of worldly appearances. In the Apocalypse of Peter, Peter is shown that Christ's physical suffering is illusory—a shadow cast for the sake of others—while his true self remains untouched. Such teachings diverge sharply from orthodox views but point to a common theme: liberation through awakening, not appeasement through sacrifice.

Many of the apocalypses included in this collection offer dazzling visions of the soul's ascent through heavenly realms. Zostrianos, Allogenes, and the Three Steles of Seth map out the spiritual terrain between the divine source and the material world, outlining complex hierarchies of aeons and intelligences. These were not idle speculations, but serious mystical attempts to chart the process by which consciousness descends into—and can ascend out of—embodied existence.

These writings are not always easy. They are dense with symbolism, laden with philosophical language, and often challenge linear reasoning. Yet they reward patient study, offering new perspectives on age-old questions: Who are we? Why is there suffering? What is the true nature of God? And how do we return to the Light from which we came?

Conflict and Suppression: Why These Writings Were Lost

The early centuries of Christianity were marked not by doctrinal unanimity, but by intense debate. Competing factions vied for authority, and many early communities read very different texts, emphasized different teachings, and lived out different spiritual practices. What we now call "orthodoxy" was one voice among many—and for much of the first three centuries, not even the dominant one.

The Gnostics, however, presented a particular threat. Their emphasis on personal revelation undermined ecclesiastical authority. Their symbolic interpretations of scripture clashed with literal readings. Their rejection of the material world ran counter to emerging sacramental theology. And their refusal to bow to dogmatic formulations made them difficult to assimilate into a hierarchical Church.

By the late 2nd and early 3rd centuries, Church Fathers such as Irenaeus, Tertullian, and Hippolytus launched aggressive campaigns against what they labeled "heresy." Lists of acceptable books began to emerge, and alternative gospels were increasingly denounced, confiscated, and destroyed. Ironically, much of what we originally knew of Gnosticism came from its enemies—who quoted the heretics in order to refute them.

That changed in 1945, when a jar of papyrus codices was discovered near Nag Hammadi in Egypt. Suddenly, the long-silenced Gnostic voices began to speak for themselves. The discovery included many of the texts now gathered in this volume: The Gospel of Truth, The Tripartite Tractate, The Apocalypse of Adam, and dozens more. For the first time in centuries, readers could explore these spiritual traditions without the filter of condemnation.

To read these texts is to step into a world of paradox, poetry, and prophecy. It is to hear the voices of mystics, philosophers, and rebels who refused to confine the divine to one set of definitions or one institutional structure. Their insights are not meant to replace canonical scripture, but to expand our understanding of the many ways human beings have encountered the divine mystery.

In reclaiming these writings, we do not just recover ancient artifacts—we open a space for contemporary exploration. In an age of spiritual disillusionment and religious plurality, the Gnostics offer not certainty, but invitation: to seek, to question, to awaken.

Let this collection serve not merely as a historical anthology, but as a spiritual companion. The journey of gnosis is as vital now as it was then—and the voices within these pages still whisper, still provoke, still call us toward the Light within.

The Gospel of Thomas

The hidden words spoken by the Savior to Judas Thomas, which I, Mathaias, wrote down as I walked with them, listening to their conversation.

The Savior said, "Brother Thomas, while you are still in this world, listen carefully to my words. I will reveal the answers to the thoughts you have kept inside. Since people say you are my twin and my true companion, take a moment to look within yourself. Learn who you really are, understand your existence, and discover how you have come to be. Since you are called my brother, you should not remain unaware of your true nature.

"I see that you have already begun to understand because you recognize that I bring the knowledge of truth. Even though you walk with me and do not yet fully comprehend everything, you have already started to know. Because of this, you will be called 'the one who knows himself.' For the person who does not know themselves knows nothing, but the one who comes to understand themselves also gains insight into the deep mysteries of all things. Therefore, my brother Thomas, you have seen what is hidden from most people—things that they stumble over in their ignorance."

Thomas replied, "Lord, I ask you to answer the questions I carry in my heart before you leave this world. When I hear you speak of hidden truths, I will be able to share them. But I realize now that understanding and living the truth is not easy for people."

The Savior answered, "If even the things you can see are unclear and confusing to you, how will you understand when I speak of things that are unseen? If the works of truth that are obvious in this world are already difficult for you to follow, how can you hope to carry out the actions that belong to the higher realms and the fullness of divine perfection, which are beyond human sight? How, then, will you be known as true 'workers' of the truth? For now, you are still like students who have not yet reached completion."

Thomas said to him, "Master, please tell us more about these things that are hidden from our understanding."

The Savior replied, "All living bodies, including animals, come into existence through natural birth. Their origins are clear, as is their nature. In the same way, the things that belong to the higher realms, though not visible in the same way, exist through their own roots. These roots produce fruit that sustains them. The bodies you see in this world, however, survive by consuming other living beings, creating a cycle of change. But this change leads to decay and death because these bodies do not hold the hope of eternal life. They are like the animals—they perish in the same way. If their origin is the same, how can they create anything different? This is why you are still like children until you reach a greater understanding."

Thomas then said, "This is why I say, Lord, that those who try to explain hidden and difficult matters are like people shooting arrows at a target in the dark. They aim and shoot as if they can see the target, but they do not truly know where it is. But when the light appears and removes the darkness, their efforts will become clear. And you, our light, reveal the truth to us, O Lord."

The Savior said, "Light finds its existence within light."

Thomas asked, "Lord, why does the light we see, which shines for people, rise and set every day?"

The Savior answered, "Thomas, this light exists for your sake—not so you can stay in this world forever, but so you can find your way out of it. When all who are chosen have turned away from their earthly desires, this light will return to its source, and its true essence will welcome it back because it has faithfully done its work."

The Savior continued, "Oh, the deep love of the true light! But also, how fierce is the fire that burns inside human bodies and bones! This fire is in them day and night, consuming their strength, clouding their thoughts, and leading their souls into confusion. It stirs up desires, both seen and unseen, pushing men toward women and women toward men.

"This is why it is said, 'Whoever seeks the truth from true wisdom must create wings for themselves so they can fly and escape the desires that control people.' He must rise above every earthly craving and free himself from the pull of the physical world."

Thomas said, "Lord, this is exactly what I want to understand, for I see that you are the one who brings true knowledge and guidance."

The Savior replied, "We must talk about these things because they are meant for those who are working toward perfection. If you want to be perfect, you must think about these truths and follow them. If you do not, then you will be called 'foolish,' for a wise person cannot live in harmony with someone who refuses to understand. A wise person grows in knowledge, while a fool sees no difference between good and bad. To the fool, they are the same. But the wise man is nourished by truth, and as the scripture says, 'He will be like a tree planted beside flowing water,' always growing and strengthened by the waters of life.

"But some, even though they have the ability to rise above, still chase after things they can see, things far from the truth. They are deceived by the fire that guides them—it looks like light, but it is only an illusion. This fire shines with a temporary beauty, attracting them with its charm. It tricks them with pleasure, trapping them in a false sense of happiness. It blinds them with endless desires, burning their souls with cravings they cannot escape. It is like a sharp stake driven into their hearts, something they cannot pull out.

"This fire, like a bridle in their mouths, controls them and steers their actions according to its will. It binds them with chains, wrapping itself around every part of them. It traps them in the suffering of wanting things that will fade away, things that constantly change and never satisfy. These people are pulled downward by their desires, consumed by them. In the end, they become like animals in this temporary world, no different from everything else that is destined to decay."

Thomas thought about this and said, "It is true, just as it is said, 'Many do not understand the truth of their own soul.'"

The Savior answered, "Blessed is the wise person who searches for truth. When he finds it, he will rest in it forever. No one will be able to shake him or make him afraid, for he will be standing on a foundation that cannot be moved."

Thomas then asked, "Lord, is it good for us to stay among people who are like us?"

The Savior said, "Yes, it is good to find peace among those who share the truth. The things people see and hold onto in this world will not last forever. Their bodies will break down and return to the earth, just like everything else that is physical. When that happens, the fire they once feared will become their suffering, fueled by their attachment to their old way of life. They will be trapped by what is visible, unable to rise beyond it.

"And those who look toward the unseen but do not truly love the truth will also perish. Their focus on worldly things will consume them, and the fire within them will destroy their souls. Soon, all that can be seen will fade away, and from its remains, only empty shadows will rise—lost souls. These souls will remain in suffering, clinging to lifeless bodies, tormented by corruption and despair."

Thomas asked, "What should we say to these people? How can we speak to those who cannot see the truth? What message should we share with those who say, 'We came to do good, not to bring curses,' yet also claim, 'If we had not been born into the flesh, we would not have known sin'?"

The Savior answered, "You must not think of such people as truly human. They are like wild animals, consuming each other with their actions. They are blind to the kingdom of light because they are drawn to the deceptive sweetness of the fire. They serve death, rushing toward corruption, following the desires of those who came before them— those who sought destruction. These people will fall into the abyss, where they will suffer the consequences of their wickedness. They will be overcome with confusion and despair, wanting to escape their own bodies but unable to do so peacefully.

"They take pleasure in their own madness without realizing it. They blindly follow their own distorted thinking, convinced they are wise. Their entire being—body, mind, and soul—is consumed by their selfish desires. They focus only on their own actions, but in the end, the fire will devour them. It will burn away their illusions, leaving them in great suffering."

Thomas asked, "Lord, what will happen to those who are cast down among them? My heart is heavy because many struggle against them."

The Savior looked at him and said, "What do you think, Thomas? What is your own understanding?"

Judas, called Thomas, answered, "Lord, it is for you to speak, and for me to listen and learn."

The Savior replied, "Then listen carefully and believe in the truth of what I say. Both the one who plants the seed and the seed itself will pass away, for everything must go through the fire. Both fire and water will consume them, and they will find themselves trapped in darkness. Over time, they will bear the bitter fruit of wickedness. Their judgment will come, and they will be destroyed by the very things they once fed— the beasts, the people, and even the forces of nature: the rain, the wind, the air, and the light above."

Thomas said, "Lord, your words have convinced us. We know in our hearts that they are true. But the world will not understand them. To them, your words will sound foolish, even laughable. How, then, can we go out and teach these things? The world does not respect us."

The Savior said, "I tell you the truth, those who hear your words but turn away in mockery, who laugh at the truth you share, will not escape judgment. Such people will be handed over to the ruler above, the one who has power over all others. This ruler will cast them down from heaven into the abyss, where they will be trapped in darkness, unable to move or escape. The depths of suffering will surround them, and there will be no forgiveness, no relief from their torment.

"The angel of punishment, Tartarouchos, will chase them, striking them with whips of fire that send sparks into their faces. No matter where they run, the fire will follow them. If they try to flee west, the flames will block their way. If they turn south, the fire will rise before them. If they go north, the burning heat will still be there. Even if they turn east, they will find no escape, for they did not seek refuge while they were alive. How will they find it when the day of judgment arrives?"

The Savior continued, "How terrible it will be for those who live without hope, who trust in things that will never come true.

"How terrible for those who put their faith in the flesh and cling to this dying world! How long will you remain blind? How long will you foolishly believe that what is eternal will also pass away? You have tied your hope to this world, and you treat this short life as your god! By doing so, you have ruined your own souls.

"How terrible for those consumed by the fire of desire, for it will never be satisfied.

"How terrible for those trapped in an endless cycle of struggle, unable to break free.

"How terrible for those who are burned by desires that destroy their bodies and poison their souls. These flames prepare them for a dreadful fate alongside others who will suffer the same."

How terrible for those who are prisoners in the darkness they have chosen! You laugh, but your laughter is empty. Your joy is wild and meaningless. You do not even realize your own downfall. You do not stop to think about your condition. You do not see that you live in darkness and walk in the shadow of death. Instead, you are consumed by the fire within you, fooled by its illusion of warmth and comfort. You have been blinded by your own desires, taking pleasure in the very things that destroy you. You find sweetness in the poison that is killing you, and you welcome the suffering caused by your own choices. You have traded freedom for chains, filling your hearts with emptiness and your minds with foolish thoughts. The fire of your own making has surrounded you with smoke, hiding the light from your eyes. You have wrapped yourselves in falsehood, trusting in things that will never last.

Do you not see that you live among those who seek to harm you? They do not see you as equals but as something to use. You have washed your souls in the water of darkness, following your desires without realizing the traps all around you. How terrible for you who have chosen lies over truth! You fail to understand that the sun, which sees everything, is watching and will one day bring justice. Even the moon sees what happens in the night and day, witnessing the actions of all people.

How terrible for those who chase after fleeting pleasures, letting their desires rule over them. How terrible for those who let their own bodies control them, for these desires will only bring suffering. How terrible for those who give in to evil spirits, letting their passions burn uncontrollably. Who will bring cool water to quench their inner fire? Who will shine a light to break the darkness inside them? Who will cleanse the polluted waters of their soul?

The sun, the moon, the air, the spirit, the earth, and the water all give life to the world. But if the sun does not shine on these things, they will dry up and die like weeds. The weeds grow wild and unchecked, choking out everything good around them. But when the grapevine is planted, it grows strong and spreads its shade over the land. It overtakes the weeds and brush, turning the soil into something rich and full of life. The vine grows healthy and full, bringing joy to its master, who no longer has to struggle against the weeds. The vine restores the land, making it fertile and abundant.

Jesus continued, saying, "How terrible for those who have rejected the truth! You work hard, but without understanding, and you rush toward your own destruction. You try to silence those who speak about life and truth, but even when you kill them, they rise again to testify against your ways.

"Blessed are those who see the dangers ahead and turn away from them.

"Blessed are those who suffer rejection and mockery because they love the Lord.

"Blessed are those who weep under the weight of suffering, for they will be set free and find peace.

"Stay alert and pray, so you do not remain trapped in the flesh. Break free from the chains of bitterness that tie you to this world. In prayer, you will find rest, leaving behind the pain and shame of this life. When you are freed from the struggles and desires of the body, you will enter the eternal rest that the Good One has prepared for you. You will reign with the King, united with him as he is with you, now and forever."

The Book of Thomas the Contender ends with this:

Remember me, my brothers and sisters, in your prayers. Peace be with the saints and with all who walk in the Spirit.

The Gospel of Mary (Magdalene)

Chapter 4

(Pages 1 to 6 of the manuscript, containing chapters 13, are lost.
The extant text starts on page 7...)

Will the physical world eventually be destroyed, or will it last forever?

The Savior answered, "Everything in nature—every form, every creature—is connected and depends on each other. But in the end, all things will return to where they came from, back to their original source. Matter itself cannot be destroyed, but it will go back to where it began. Each part of creation is naturally drawn back to its own origin, and when it returns, it becomes whole again."

Then He said, "If you have ears, listen carefully and understand."

Peter, wanting to learn more, asked, "Since you have taught us so much, please tell us this: What is the sin of the world?"

The Savior replied, "Sin is not something that was placed on the world. It is not an outside force—it comes from human actions. Sin happens when people go against their true nature, when they act in ways that are not in harmony with how things were meant to be. This is why acts like adultery are considered sin—they are not part of the original design."

He continued, "The Good has entered the world to restore everything to its rightful place. That is the purpose of divine intervention—to bring all things back to where they belong, to heal what is broken, and to recover what was lost.

"This is also why people get sick and die. You are missing the presence of the One who has the power to heal you. When you lose that connection, you are separated from the source of life."

He added, "If you have the mind to understand, think deeply about these truths."

The Savior then explained further, "Matter itself gave rise to desires that were never meant to exist. These desires create chaos and disrupt the natural order. They bring disorder to all of creation. That is why I have told you, 'Do not be afraid.' And when you do feel discouraged, find strength in the beauty and balance of nature. Everything is part of a greater design, and in the end, all things will return to harmony."

Once more, He said, "If you have ears, truly listen and understand."

When the Blessed One finished teaching, He spoke with deep peace, saying, "Peace be with you. Take my peace into your hearts and carry it within you. Be careful of those who try to mislead you by saying, 'Look over here!' or 'Look over there!' The Son of Man is not found in such places. He is within you. Seek Him inside yourself, for those who truly look for Him will find Him."

The Savior then told them, "Go and share the good news of the Kingdom. Tell this truth to everyone who will listen. Do not create extra rules or burdens beyond what I have taught you. Do not set up laws like the old lawgivers did, or you will trap yourselves and others with unnecessary restrictions. The path I have given you is enough."

After saying this, He left them, filling them with peace and the wisdom of His words.

Chapter 5

The disciples were filled with sorrow. Their hearts felt heavy as they cried and mourned, saying, "How can we go out and share the message of the Son of Man with those who do not know Him? If they did not spare Him, our Savior, why would they treat us any differently? Surely, we will suffer just as He did."

Then Mary stood up among them, her presence strong and steady. She greeted them warmly and said, "My brothers, do not weep, and do not let grief take over your hearts. Do not lose hope or let fear stop you. The grace of the Savior will stay with you. It will protect you and guide you in the mission He has given you."

She continued, "Instead of focusing on sorrow, let us give thanks and praise for all He has done. He has prepared us for this. He has changed us, making us strong so that we can continue His work."

Her words brought them comfort, and as she spoke, their sadness began to fade. The disciples felt their hearts turning back toward the truth. They started to reflect on the Savior's teachings, feeling a new sense of purpose.

Peter then turned to Mary and said, "Sister, we know that the Savior thought highly of you, that He loved you more than the other women. You understand His teachings more deeply than we do. Please, share with us what He told you—things that we have not heard. Teach us what has been hidden from us."

Mary, calm and confident, replied, "What you do not know, I will now reveal to you. These are the things I have kept close to my heart, and I will share them so that you too may understand."

She then began to speak. "I saw the Lord in a vision. I said to Him, 'Lord, today I saw You in a vision.' He answered me, 'Blessed are you,

Mary, because you believed what you saw without doubting. Where your mind is focused, there your treasure will also be.'"

I asked Him, 'Lord, when someone sees a vision, how do they perceive it? Through the soul, or through the spirit?'

The Savior replied, 'It is not through the soul or the spirit that visions are seen. It is through the mind, which exists between the two. The mind is like a bridge, connecting what is seen to what is understood. Through it, true wisdom is revealed.'"

Mary paused, her words carrying deep meaning. The disciples sat in silence, reflecting on what she had shared, trying to grasp the mystery of her vision and the wisdom of the Savior's teaching.

(pages 1114 are missing from the manuscript)

Chapter 8

Desire confronted the soul and said, "I didn't see you when you first entered the world, but now I see you leaving it. Why are you trying to trick me? You belong to me—you always have."

But the soul stood firm and replied, "I saw you, but you never truly saw me or understood who I am. I wrapped myself around you like a garment, covering you, but you never recognized my purpose or my presence."

After saying this, the soul moved forward, filled with joy and victory.

As it ascended, the soul encountered the third force, Ignorance. This power blocked its way and demanded, "Where do you think you're going? You are trapped in darkness and cannot escape. You are bound by sin, so you have no right to judge."

The soul replied with confidence, "Why do you accuse me when I have judged no one? I was trapped by forces I did not choose, but I have never trapped anyone. You did not recognize me, but I have come to recognize you. Now I see that everything—the heavens and the earth—is returning to its true source."

Having overcome Ignorance, the soul gained even more strength and determination. It then came upon the fourth power, a great force that appeared in seven different forms:

1. Darkness, blinding the way and creating fear.

2. Desire, overwhelming and consuming.

3. Ignorance, spreading confusion and doubt.

4. Fear of death, shaking the soul with terror.

5. The rule of the flesh, tempting with worldly pleasures.

6. False wisdom, pretending to hold knowledge but offering nothing.

7. Anger and pride, burning with destruction and arrogance.

These seven forces together made up the power of Wrath, standing in the soul's path to challenge its journey.

They spoke, accusing the soul, "Where do you come from, you who have defied us? And where do you think you are going? You dare to rise above the powers that rule this world?"

The soul stood strong and answered without fear, "The things that once held me back have no power over me anymore. I have overcome them. My desires have faded, and ignorance has been destroyed."

The soul continued, "I no longer belong to this world. I am free from the chains of illusion and forgetfulness that once kept me trapped. These things are temporary, but I am not. Now, I will rise to a place of eternal peace, a realm beyond time, where everything is whole and unchanging."

With these words, the soul broke free from the grasp of the powers, rising beyond their reach. It entered the eternal light, where it finally found true rest.

Chapter 9

When Mary finished speaking, she became silent because that was all the Savior had shared with her.

But Andrew turned to the others and said, "Say what you think about what she just said. But I don't believe the Savior actually said this. These ideas seem strange to me."

Then Peter also spoke, responding to the same discussion.

He questioned them, saying, "Could the Savior really have spoken privately with a woman and not to us? Are we supposed to listen to her now? Did He really choose her over us?"

Mary started to cry and said to Peter, "My brother Peter, do you really think I made this up? Do you believe I am lying about what the Savior said?"

Levi then spoke up and said to Peter, "Peter, you have always been quick to anger."

"Now I see you attacking this woman just like our enemies would."

"But if the Savior considered her worthy, who are you to reject her? Surely, He knows her well."

"That is why He loved her more than us. Instead of arguing, we should be ashamed of our doubts and focus on becoming the true people He called us to be. Let's go our separate ways as He commanded and preach the gospel, without adding any extra rules or laws beyond what the Savior taught."

After hearing this, they went out and began spreading His message.

The Gospel of Philip

A Hebrew welcomes another Hebrew into their community, calling them a "proselyte." However, while a proselyte can join the group, they cannot bring in another proselyte themselves. They remain as they are, shaped by those who accepted them, but they do not continue the cycle by bringing in others. Some people are creators and builders, while others simply exist without shaping or changing anything.

A slave longs for freedom, but even in their desire to be free, they do not expect to inherit their master's estate. A son, on the other hand, not only knows he is a son but also has a rightful claim to his father's inheritance. Those who inherit from what is dead are also bound to death, as they receive nothing but lifeless things. But those who inherit from what is truly alive gain both life and the inheritance of both the living and the dead. The dead cannot inherit anything, for how can something without life receive anything at all? Yet, if the dead were to inherit what is alive, they would no longer remain dead but would instead become fully alive.

A Gentile does not experience death in the same way as others because they were never truly alive to begin with. However, the one who believes in the truth has found real life. This new life also makes them vulnerable to death because only those who are alive can die. Since Christ came, the world has been changed—its cities transformed, and the dead brought out into the open. When we were Hebrews, we were like orphans, with only a mother to care for us. But when we became Christians, we gained both a father and a mother, becoming part of a divine family.

A person who plants seeds in winter will harvest their crops in summer. Winter represents this present world, while summer symbolizes the eternal realm. So, we should plant our seeds now in this life so we can reap the rewards of eternity. That is why we should not focus only on prayer in this world but also on what is to come. Just as summer follows winter, the eternal realm follows this temporary one. If someone tries to harvest in winter, they will not gather anything ripe—only unformed, useless crops. Just as barren land in winter cannot bring forth a full harvest, the Sabbath, without proper preparation, cannot bring life.

Christ came with a mission: to set some people free, to save others, and to redeem many. He ransomed those who were far from him, bringing them into his family. He saved those he had chosen, and he redeemed them according to his plan. His sacrifice did not begin at the moment of his arrival on earth; rather, he had been giving himself up willingly since the foundation of the world. When he came into the world, it was to reclaim what had already been his. That which belonged to him had fallen into the hands of thieves and been taken captive, but Christ came to rescue it. Through his sacrifice, he redeemed both the good and the evil in the world, leaving no one outside the reach of his grace.

Light and darkness, life and death, right and left—these opposites are connected, like siblings. They exist together, inseparable. Because of this, we must understand that good is not entirely good, nor is evil entirely evil. Life itself is not fully alive, and death is not completely dead. Everything will eventually return to where it came from. However, those who have risen above the contradictions of this world will not dissolve—they are eternal.

The words we use to describe things in this world can be misleading. They often take our thoughts in the wrong direction, distracting us from the truth. For example, when someone hears the word "God," they do not immediately grasp the full reality of who He is. Instead, they hold onto an imperfect idea. The same is true for words like "Father," "Son," "Holy Spirit," "life," "light," "resurrection," and "the Church." These words can be misunderstood unless someone truly understands the deeper meaning behind them. The names we use in this world are part of this world; they are not eternal. If they belonged to the eternal realm, they would not be expressed in the flawed language of this world. Eventually, these names will disappear when the eternal realm is fully revealed.

But there is one name that is not spoken in this world—the name that the Father gave to the Son. This name is greater than all names and fully expresses the Father's essence. The Son becomes one with the Father through this name. Those who have received it know it deeply, but they do not say it aloud. Those who have not received it remain unaware of its true power.

Truth gave names to things in the world so that we could understand them. Without names, learning would be impossible. Even though truth is one, it appears in many different forms so that we can recognize it. These names are used with love, helping us see how everything is connected to the same truth. However, the rulers of this world saw that humans were linked to what is truly good, and they wanted to deceive us. So, they took the names of what is good and attached them to things that were not good, hoping to confuse people and keep them under their control. But their trick ended up helping in an unexpected way. By creating lies, they forced people to search for what is real, making it easier to tell truth from falsehood and put everything in its rightful place.

The rulers of this world do not want humanity to be saved. They want to stay in power because if people find salvation, they will no longer need to offer sacrifices, which is what gives these rulers their strength. The animals placed on their altars were sacrifices meant for the rulers themselves—living creatures that were killed in the offering. But humanity was different. People were offered up in death, only to be given eternal life in return.

Before Christ came, the world did not have the true bread of life. It was like the Garden of Eden, where Adam lived. That garden had many trees that fed the animals, but it had no wheat to nourish human beings. In those times, people ate as animals did, without anything greater to lift them above their natural instincts. But when Christ arrived as the perfect human, he brought the true bread from heaven. This was not physical food, but spiritual nourishment, meant to feed the soul and help people rise above earthly things.

The rulers of the world believed they were acting on their own power, making choices freely. But in reality, the Holy Spirit was guiding everything, turning their actions into part of a greater divine plan. Truth, which has existed since the very beginning, is like a seed scattered throughout the world. Many people see it being planted, but only a few truly understand its purpose. The mystery of truth remains hidden from those who are not ready to receive it.

Some people have said, "Mary conceived by the Holy Spirit." But they misunderstand the deeper meaning of this mystery. When has a woman ever conceived a child through another woman? Mary is a pure and untouched virgin, undefiled by any power. Her role is a deep mystery and a challenge even to the Hebrews, including the apostles and their followers. She represents something beyond corruption, proving that the rulers of this world have no control over her. When Jesus spoke of "My Father who is in Heaven," he said it this way because he has another Father beyond the earthly one. If he had only meant an earthly father, he would have simply said, "My Father."

The Lord told his disciples, "Go out and gather people from every household, bringing them into the house of the Father. But take nothing from the house of the Father and do not carry anything away."

The name "Jesus" is mysterious and hidden, while "Christ" is a name that has been revealed. The name "Jesus" remains the same in every language, but "Christ" changes based on the language being spoken. In Syriac, it is "Messiah," and in Greek, it is "Christos." Every culture has its own way of saying it. "The Nazarene" is the one who makes hidden things visible. Christ contains everything—humanity, angels, mysteries, and even the Father himself.

Some people mistakenly say that the Lord died before he rose. But this is not true. He rose first and then died. To truly understand death, one must first experience resurrection. For as God lives, life comes before all things.

Think of it this way: No one hides a great treasure in a large, obvious place. Instead, valuable riches are often stored inside something small and ordinary. In the same way, the soul is a precious jewel, hidden within the human body, which may seem simple on the outside but holds something far greater within.

Many people are afraid of rising in the resurrection without a body, so they insist that they will rise in the flesh. But they don't understand that having flesh is actually a form of being naked. The ones who remove their earthly bodies are the ones who are truly clothed. "Flesh and blood cannot inherit the kingdom of God." What does this mean? It refers to our physical bodies, which are temporary. But what will enter the kingdom? Only what belongs to Jesus—his true flesh and blood. His flesh is the Word, and his blood is the Holy Spirit. Those who receive these will have eternal nourishment, drink, and clothing.

Some say that the flesh will not rise, while others insist that it will.

Both are mistaken. To truly rise, one must go beyond the physical body, for everything already exists within it. In this world, people are more important than the clothes they wear. But in the kingdom of heaven, the garments of the soul are greater than the ones who wear them.

Everything is purified by water and fire. What we see is cleansed by visible things, and what is hidden is cleansed by invisible forces. Just as water exists within water, fire is present within the sacred anointing oil.

Jesus revealed himself to everyone in different ways, appearing in a form they could understand. To those who were great, he appeared as great. To those who were small, he appeared as small. To angels, he looked like an angel. To humans, he appeared as a man. Because of this, many did not truly recognize him; they only saw a reflection of themselves. But when he took his disciples up the mountain and revealed his true glory, he appeared in his full greatness, and they were made great enough to see him.

On that day, he gave thanks, saying, "You who have united the perfect light with the Holy Spirit, let the angels join us as reflections of that perfection."

Do not look down on the lamb, for it is the way to the king. No one can approach the king without it, and no one can enter his presence without being clothed.

The heavenly man has far more children than the earthly man. If the children of Adam are many, even though they die, how much greater are the children of the perfect man, who live forever. A father creates a son, but a son does not create another son; instead, he gains brothers. In this world, all are born in a natural way, but they are nourished by their true origin.

It is through the promise of heaven that humanity is sustained. The Word, which comes from that place, feeds the soul and leads it to perfection. The perfect ones give life through a kiss. That is why we greet one another with a kiss, sharing the grace that lives within us.

Three women always walked with the Lord: Mary, his mother; her sister; and Mary Magdalene, his companion. Each of them was called Mary, but each had a unique role in his life.

"The Father" and "the Son" are single names, but "the Holy Spirit" is a double name. It exists both above and below, in both what is seen and what is hidden. The Holy Spirit moves between both realms, connecting what is secret with what is revealed.

Without knowing it, the saints are sometimes served by evil powers. These powers are blinded by the Holy Spirit, making them think they are serving ordinary humans when they are actually serving the saints.

Once, a disciple asked the Lord for something of this world. The Lord replied, "Ask your mother, and she will give you what belongs to someone else."

The apostles said to the disciples, "May our offering be seasoned with salt so that it may be pleasing." They referred to wisdom as "salt," because without it, an offering would not be accepted. Wisdom does not bear children, and because of this, she is called "a trace of salt." But her barrenness does not mean she has no influence. Wherever she is present, the Holy Spirit moves, multiplying her children and making them many.

What the Father has also belongs to the Son. But as long as the Son is still a child, he is not given full authority over it. Only when he matures does the Father entrust him with everything, giving him his full inheritance.

Those who go astray or are led astray by the Spirit often fall because of that same Spirit. This is the mystery of its power: it can start a fire, and it can put one out, depending on its purpose.

Echamoth and Echmoth may sound similar, but they are not the same. Echamoth represents true wisdom—the divine knowledge that brings light and understanding. Echmoth, however, is the wisdom of death, tied to the knowledge of the physical world and everything that fades away. It is called "the little wisdom" because it belongs to things that do not last.

Think about the animals in the world. Some, like oxen and donkeys, live alongside people and help with work. Others are wild, roaming freely in deserts and forests. Farmers use domesticated animals to plow fields, and through their labor, both people and animals are fed. Even the wild animals benefit in some way from the land that is cultivated.

In the same way, the perfect man works in harmony with the forces that follow him, preparing everything for its purpose. Through this balance, everything in creation—both good and bad—exists together. The Holy Spirit watches over all things, guiding both the tame and the wild, ensuring that everything, even those who try to escape, remains within God's plan.

Creation reflects its source. Something that is created can be beautiful, but its offspring are not always noble. If something were begotten instead of made, its children would carry true nobility. But when something created gives birth, its offspring lack the full measure of divine greatness. This can be seen in the first acts of wrongdoing—adultery came first, and then from it, murder. The one born of adultery, the child of the serpent, became a murderer, taking his own brother's life. Every time two things that do not belong together are joined, it distorts the harmony of creation.

God is like a master dyer. Just as a cloth is dipped into dye and takes on its color, so God colors the soul with his eternal spirit. Those who are dyed in God's colors become immortal, for his colors never fade. He purifies his chosen ones, making them shine with his divine presence.

To truly see something, you must become like it. In the physical world, you can see the sun, the sky, the earth, and everything around you without becoming them. But in the higher realms, seeing and becoming are the same. When you see the Spirit, you become spirit. When you see Christ, you become like Christ. When you see the Father, you become one with him. In this vision, you are no longer separate; you merge with what you behold.

Faith is how we receive, and love is how we give. Without faith, a person cannot receive anything of true value. Without love, they cannot give in a way that matters. We believe so that we may receive, and we give out of love. Giving without love is empty—it is just an action without meaning. Those who receive anything apart from the Lord remain attached to the old ways, unable to rise above their earthly identity.

The apostles before us called him "Jesus the Nazorean, the Messiah," meaning "Jesus the Nazorean, the Christ." These names reveal who he is. "Jesus" in Hebrew means "salvation." "Nazara" means "truth," and "the Nazarene" represents the very essence of truth. "Christ" means "the anointed one," signifying someone chosen and set apart for a divine purpose.

A pearl may be tossed into the mud and ignored, but its value does not change in the eyes of its owner. In the same way, the children of God always remain valuable, no matter where they are, for their Father always knows their worth.

If you call yourself a Jew, a Roman, a Greek, or a servant, no one will be disturbed. But if you say, "I am a Christian," the powers of the world will tremble. Just speaking this name unsettles the forces of darkness because it carries the authority of God.

God is like a "man-eater," receiving the sacrifices of humanity. Before people were offered as sacrifices, animals were given, because those who received them were not truly gods.

Both glass and clay pots are shaped by fire. If a glass vessel breaks, it can be melted down and reshaped, because it was formed through the breath of creation. But if a clay pot shatters, it is lost forever, because it lacks that same breath.

A donkey that walks in circles grinding grain may travel for miles, yet it never leaves the same spot. In the same way, some people work hard their entire lives but never move forward in what truly matters. At the end of all their efforts, they realize they have gained nothing—they have seen neither the works of man nor the wonders of God. Their labor has led them nowhere.

The eucharist represents Christ himself. In Syriac, he is called "Pharisatha," meaning "the one who is spread out," because he was stretched upon the cross to bring salvation to the world.

The Lord visited the dye works of Levi, where fabrics were colored using seventy-two different dyes. He took them all and placed them in a single vat. When he pulled them out, every fabric was pure white. He said, "Just as I have made all these colors one, the Son of Man has come to purify and unite all things."

Wisdom, often called barren, is the mother of angels. Mary Magdalene, who was close to Jesus, was loved by him more than the other disciples. He often kissed her on the lips, a sign of divine closeness. The disciples, seeing this, asked, "Why do you love her more than us?"

Jesus answered, "Why do you think I love her more than you? When a blind person and one who can see are in darkness, they are the same. But when the light comes, the one who sees will recognize it, while the blind will remain in darkness."

The Lord said, "Blessed is the one who existed before being born, for such a person is eternal and not bound by time. The eternal one has always been, is now, and always will be."

The greatness of a person is not something you can see with your eyes. It lies within. This hidden strength gives people mastery over animals, which may be physically stronger but lack understanding. Through wisdom, humans bring order to the wild. Without them, animals turn on each other, fighting and killing without purpose. It is man's labor—working the land and caring for the earth—that provides food and sustains life. Without this effort, nature remains in chaos.

If someone is baptized but does not receive the Holy Spirit, then calls themselves a Christian, they are only borrowing the name. They have taken on the title, but it comes with a responsibility they have not fulfilled. However, the one who truly receives the Holy Spirit does not borrow the name—it is given to them as a gift. A true gift requires no repayment, only acceptance. This is the difference between someone who has only claimed faith and someone who has truly been transformed by God's grace.

Marriage is a deep and sacred mystery. Without it, the world would not exist. The union of male and female continues life and reflects a divine truth. The existence of everything depends on this mystery, and within it lies great power. Yet, in the physical world, relationships are often flawed, and instead of reflecting divine unity, they sometimes reveal human weakness.

Evil spirits also take different forms—both male and female—

seeking to corrupt what they can. Male spirits attach themselves to female souls, and female spirits attach themselves to male souls, taking advantage of those who are unguarded or disobedient. These spirits can only be overcome through divine power, which is given through the unity of the bridegroom and the bride, a symbol of the connection between God and the soul.

When lustful women see a man sitting alone, they approach him to lead him into temptation. In the same way, when corrupt men see a woman alone, they seek to take advantage of her. But when a man and woman are together in unity, neither male nor female spirits can harm them. This unity is a reflection of the sacred connection between the divine image and the angelic presence, which cannot be broken.

A person who rises above the world and no longer craves its temptations cannot be controlled by the forces that once held them back. They are beyond jealousy, fear, and temptation. But those who are still tied to the world remain vulnerable. If evil spirits come, they will take hold of a soul that does not have the Holy Spirit. Only those filled with the Spirit are safe, because no unclean force can touch them.

Do not be afraid of the body, but do not love it too much either. If you fear it, it will rule over you. If you love it too much, you will be trapped by it. The body is only a temporary covering, and being too attached to it keeps the soul from being free.

A person can be in one of three states: in the world, in resurrection, or stuck in between. No one should be caught in the middle! The world has both good and bad, but even the good in this world is not perfect, and the bad is not completely evil. However, the middle state—what some call death—is entirely empty and separated from God.

While we are alive, we should seek the resurrection. To enter resurrection means to prepare the soul for rest, to leave behind the body, and to rise above the state of being stuck between life and eternal light. Many people lose their way and become trapped in the middle, unable to move forward. It is better to leave this world in purity before sin takes hold, because the resurrection brings peace and unity with God. The middle place is a state of wandering, where the soul is neither fully in the world nor in the light.

We should strive to leave this world with grace, walking the path of righteousness. Then, when we leave our bodies behind, we can enter the eternal peace of resurrection instead of being lost in the middle. Those who walk this path overcome fear, sin, and death, finding unity with God forever.

Some people lack both the desire and the ability to do what is right. Others may have the will but do nothing. Neither is enough. In both cases, they fail because justice requires both desire and action together.

One of the apostles had a vision of people trapped in a burning house, bound by chains of fire. The flames surrounded them, and they cried out in pain and despair. Their faith had failed them. The apostle asked, "Why are you here? Can't you be saved?" They answered, "We never wanted to be saved. When salvation was offered, we ignored it. Now we suffer in the darkness because of our own choices."

The soul and spirit were created through water and fire, two of the essential elements of life. But the son of the bridal chamber was born through water, fire, and light. This fire is not destructive but pure and bright. It is the light that reveals all things.

Truth did not come into the world in its pure form because people were not ready to accept it. Instead, it was revealed through symbols and images. Even rebirth is hidden in imagery. To be reborn, a person must pass through the symbol of rebirth, which is resurrection. The image of resurrection must lead to the image of truth. The mysteries of the bridal chamber must also pass through these images before they can restore what was lost.

Those who speak of the Father, the Son, and the Holy Spirit must not just say the names but live by their truth. If they do not, even the title of "Christian" will be taken from them. One must receive the power of the cross, which the apostles described as "the right and the left."

A person who reaches this level is no longer just a follower of Christ—they become like Christ himself.

The Lord carried out everything with deep meaning: baptism, anointing, communion, salvation, and the sacred union. He said, "I came to make the things on earth reflect what is in heaven, to bring the outside and the inside together, and to create harmony in all things." His actions were filled with symbols and images, guiding people toward the full truth.

Some say, "There is a heavenly man, and another above him." This is incorrect. The first heavenly man, the one we see, is wrongly considered "lower," while the hidden one is thought to be "higher." A better way to describe it is "the inner, the outer, and what lies beyond the outer," because beyond the outermost darkness, nothing exists. The Lord called it "the outer darkness" because it is complete emptiness. He spoke of "My Father who is in secret" and taught, "Go into your room, close the door, and pray to your Father in secret," because the Father is present within all things.

Before Christ came, some people had left a place they could never return to, while others had entered a place they could never escape. Christ came to change this: he freed those who were trapped and brought home those who were lost.

When Eve stayed with Adam, there was no death. It was only when she separated from him that death began. If they reunite and become one again, death will come to an end.

On the cross, Christ cried out, "My God, my God, why have you abandoned me?" This marked the moment he left the earthly world to complete his divine mission.

A sacred union is not meant for animals, slaves, or those who are unclean. It is for those who are free and pure in spirit. Through the Holy Spirit, we are born again, and through Christ, we are anointed and made whole.

When we are reborn, we are joined together in the light and water of baptism. Light reveals truth, but it cannot be seen without something to reflect it, like a mirror or water. That is why baptism includes both light and water, with anointing as the light that cleanses and reveals.

In Jerusalem, three buildings were used for sacrifices. The western one was called "The Holy," the southern was "The Holy of the Holy," and the eastern was "The Holy of the Holies," which only the high priest could enter. Baptism is like "The Holy," resurrection is like "The Holy of the Holy," and the sacred union is like "The Holy of the Holies." The veil separating the sacred union was torn from top to bottom so that those below could rise up to the highest place.

The rulers of this world cannot see those who are clothed in perfect light, because the light protects them from harm. Those who are united in this light are free from the grasp of worldly powers.

If the woman had never been separated from the man, she would not have died. Separation was the beginning of death. Christ came to heal this division, bringing back together what was broken and restoring life to those who had been lost.

The union of man and woman in the sacred bond brings eternal unity, ensuring they will never be separated again. Eve was divided from Adam because she was joined to him outside this sacred bond. Christ came to restore this union in truth, offering eternal life to those who are united in it.

Adam's soul was given to him through God's breath, filling him with life. His true partner was the spirit, a divine gift meant to complete him. The earth, which was his mother, gave him a body to carry his soul. But later, his soul was replaced by the spirit, transforming him in ways that the rulers of the world could not understand. When Adam united with the spirit, he spoke words that went beyond human understanding. The rulers of the world became jealous because his connection to the spirit allowed him to understand mysteries they could not grasp. His spiritual partner was hidden from them, kept in a sacred space just for him—like a secret chamber that protected their union from corruption.

When Jesus arrived at the Jordan River, he brought with him the fullness of God's kingdom. He, who existed before all things, was born again. He, who had already been anointed, received a new anointing. He, who had been redeemed, became the one who would redeem others. His coming fulfilled a great divine mystery, bringing renewal to everything.

It is said that the Father of all united with a pure spirit that came down from above. On that day, a great light appeared, shining over the sacred place of divine union. From this, the body of Christ was formed—born from the holy bond between the bridegroom and the bride. Through this, Jesus established everything within the sacred union, a place of eternal peace and divine connection. Because of this, every disciple is called to enter that peace and take part in the unity that was destined from the beginning.

Adam was also created from two pure sources: the Spirit and the untouched earth. Christ, who was born of a virgin, came to undo the mistake that began with Adam's fall. He restored what was lost and repaired the separation between people and God.

In Paradise, there were two trees. One gave birth to animals, and the other gave birth to people. Adam, following his desires, ate from the tree that produced animals. By doing this, he became like them and passed on that nature to his children. Because of this, Adam's descendants began to worship animals, treating them as gods. But there was another tree—the one that created true people, made in God's image. This tree bore the fruit of life, but Adam never ate from it. This is similar to how people create their own gods and worship them, instead of realizing that it is the divine that should recognize humans as its creators.

A person's success depends on their abilities, and their achievements are the result of their hard work. One of their greatest achievements is their children, yet they are created not through struggle but through ease. This reflects a deeper truth: just as people work hard to build and create, their children are formed effortlessly. This mystery mirrors something greater about the nature of the divine.

In this world, slaves serve the free, following the natural order of society. But in the Kingdom of Heaven, the free will serve the slaves. Those who have entered the sacred union—the children of the bridal chamber—will care for those still tied to the world. The children of the bridal chamber have only one purpose: rest. They do not need anything else because they exist in divine peace, beyond the need for change or transformation.

When someone enters the waters of baptism and rises again, their faith makes the water sacred. Baptism is not just a ritual—it is the fulfillment of righteousness, just as Jesus said: "This is how we fulfill all righteousness."

Some people believe they will die first and then rise again, but they are mistaken. If someone does not experience resurrection while they are alive, they will gain nothing after death. Baptism is not just about being cleansed—it is a great mystery of life. Those who receive it with faith gain eternal life, because baptism is a direct connection to resurrection.

The soul, spirit, and body are all connected in creation and salvation. Just as Adam's soul was later replaced by a spirit, each person must seek the divine unity that restores them to their true nature. Through baptism, resurrection, and the sacred union, people are given a path beyond the limits of this world, leading them into the eternal peace promised by Christ.

Philip the apostle once explained, "Joseph the carpenter planted a garden, needing wood for his work. From the trees he planted, he built the cross. And on that very cross, his own descendant hung. That descendant was Jesus, and the tree he planted became the cross itself." The Tree of Life stands at the center of the garden, but it was the olive tree that gave us the sacred oil. Through this oil, we receive resurrection and renewal, linking us to the divine.

This world consumes the dead, for it is a devourer of lifeless things. Everything it takes in eventually dies. But truth consumes what is living, and instead of death, it gives eternal nourishment. Those who are fed by truth will never die. Jesus came from this eternal place and brought divine food. To those who hungered for it, he gave life so they would never taste death.

God created a garden and placed man inside it. In this garden, choices had to be made, but there were also rules: "Eat this, but do not eat that." However, in the higher garden, where divine fulfillment exists, the rules are different. There, people freely eat from the Tree of Knowledge—not to bring death, but to receive life. In the lower garden, the Tree of Knowledge led to death. The law, represented by that tree, taught people about good and evil, but it didn't lead them toward goodness or keep them from evil. Instead, it brought death because the command "Eat this, don't eat that" became the very thing that caused mankind to fall.

The sacred oil, known as chrism, is greater than baptism. We are called "Christians" because of the chrism, not baptism. The name "Christ" itself comes from this anointing. The Father anointed the Son, the Son anointed the apostles, and the apostles anointed us. Those who are anointed receive everything—resurrection, the light, the cross, and the Holy Spirit. These gifts are given in the sacred place of divine union. The Father and Son are united, with the Father in the Son and the Son in the Father. This is the Kingdom of Heaven, a place of unity and fulfillment.

Jesus spoke truthfully when he said, "Some entered the Kingdom of Heaven laughing, yet came out serious." Why? Because they rejected the world and its distractions, realizing how meaningless they were. When they entered the water, they left behind everything that tied them to the world and rose into something greater. If someone despises the world and sees it as unimportant, they come out of the water joyful, having received the peace of the Kingdom of Heaven. The same is true for the sacred bread, the cup, and the oil, though there is something even greater that awaits the faithful.

The world itself was created through a mistake. Its creator wanted to make it perfect and immortal but failed. Neither the world nor its maker will last forever. True eternal life belongs only to the children of God. Nothing can receive eternal life unless it first becomes a child of

God, and one who does not have eternity within them cannot give it to others.

The cup of prayer holds wine and water, representing the blood of Christ for which people give thanks. This cup is filled with the Holy Spirit and belongs to those who have been made whole. Drinking from it allows people to receive the true life of Christ, taking on his essence. Before someone enters the water, they remove their old clothing, symbolizing the shedding of their mortal nature. Only then can they be clothed in the new life and receive eternity.

Just as a horse gives birth to horses and a man fathers children, a god brings forth gods. The bridegroom and the bride share this divine origin. They come from a sacred lineage that is not divided by the labels of this world. Before this origin, there was no Jew or Gentile—those who belong to the eternal realm are part of the true people, the children of the divine light.

In this world, relationships often have imbalance, with the husband's strength complementing the wife's perceived weakness. But in the eternal realm, these limitations do not exist. The unions there are greater than any in this world. They do not separate into different roles but exist as one, beyond the limits of flesh and mortality.

Those who have everything must know themselves. Without self-knowledge, they cannot truly enjoy their inheritance. But those who understand themselves will find joy and fulfillment in all they have because true understanding is the key to experiencing life in its fullest form.

The perfect person cannot be captured or even seen by the powers of this world. If they were seen, the powers would try to take hold of them, but they cannot grasp someone who is clothed in perfect light. To reach this state, a person must become light themselves, entering divine unity. Only then can they rise beyond the limitations of this world and leave behind the imperfection of the middle place, stepping fully into the eternal realm.

A priest is a sacred vessel, and everything he touches becomes holy. If he blesses the bread or the cup, how much more is his own body made holy, reflecting the divine presence within him?

Through baptism, Jesus removed death's hold. When we enter the waters, we no longer enter death—we rise into new life. We are no longer trapped by the spirit of this world that brings the coldness of despair. Instead, when the Holy Spirit moves over us, it brings the warmth of renewal, filling us with the life of eternity.

The one who truly knows the truth is a free person. But this freedom is not shallow or worldly, because the free person does not live in sin. As it is written, "Anyone who sins is a slave to sin" (John 8:34). Truth is like a nurturing mother, and knowledge is like a guiding father. Together, they bring forth freedom and true understanding.

Some people believe that sin does not apply to them, and the world calls them "free." But this so-called freedom, based only on knowledge, often makes them proud. This is why it is said, "it makes them free." They feel above others, as if they have risen beyond the world. But knowledge alone is not enough. As it is written, "Love builds up" (1 Corinthians 8:1). True freedom does not come from knowledge alone but from knowledge combined with love.

Someone who is truly free, through deep understanding, chooses to serve others out of love—especially those who have not yet found freedom. Knowledge gives a person the ability to be free, but love connects them to others. Love does not separate or claim ownership, saying, "This belongs to me, and that belongs to you." Instead, love says, "Everything is yours."

Spiritual love is like the finest wine or the most fragrant oil. When a person is anointed with it, they feel joy and fulfillment. The fragrance of love benefits not only the one who carries it but also those around them. When a person filled with love is present, everyone nearby experiences its goodness. But if that person leaves, those who remain return to their original state, lacking that fragrance. This is like the Samaritan who poured wine and oil on the wounds of an injured man. The wine and oil were not just physical substances—they symbolized love and healing. As it is written, "Love covers a multitude of sins" (1 Peter 4:8).

The children a woman gives birth to often resemble the one who loves her. If her husband loves her, the children will look like him. But if she gives her heart to another man—someone who is not her husband—the children may carry his likeness instead. Even if she stays with her husband out of duty, her longing for someone else may influence the children she bears. In the same way, if you live with the Son of God, do not love the world, but love the Lord. If you do, the spiritual life you bring forth will reflect the Lord, not the broken image of the world.

In all creation, beings naturally connect with their own kind. Humans gather with humans, horses stay with horses, and so on. This reflects a deeper truth: spirit joins with spirit, thought connects with thought, and light unites with light. If you remain human in nature, people will embrace you. But if you rise to a higher level and become spirit, then spirit will unite with you. If you become pure thought, thought will blend with you. If you become light, light will shine within you. Those who belong to the divine realm will rest upon you if you align yourself with them.

But if you lower yourself to the level of an animal—acting like a horse, a donkey, a bull, or a dog—then neither humanity, spirit, thought, nor light will connect with you. Neither those from above nor those from within will recognize or rest in you. In this state, you will have no part in what is divine or eternal.

A slave who is forced into servitude may one day be freed. But someone who was set free by their master's kindness and then willingly returns to slavery may never be freed again. This is the great loss of someone who turns away from the freedom they were given.

Farming in the natural world requires balance among four key elements: water, earth, wind, and light. Only when these elements work together can the harvest be gathered into the barn. In the same way, God's spiritual work depends on four things: faith, hope, love, and knowledge. Faith is like the earth, providing the foundation where we grow. Hope is like water, sustaining and strengthening us. Love is like the wind, helping us grow and expand. Knowledge is like the light, guiding us toward full maturity.

Grace is shown in four ways: it comes from the earth, descends from heaven, reaches the highest places, and extends beyond what we can understand. These forces work together, just like the elements of nature support life.

Through these mysteries, we learn that knowledge alone cannot bring true freedom without love. Real freedom doesn't come from pride in what we know but from humility in serving others and connecting with the divine. Love moves like the wind, and knowledge shines like light, helping the soul grow until it is ready to take its place in eternity.

Blessed is the person who has never caused harm or suffering to another soul. Such a person is truly like Christ. Jesus himself lived this way—he brought light and comfort without adding burdens to anyone. He was the perfect man, but perfection is difficult for us to define.

How can we, who are imperfect, reach such greatness? How can we bring comfort to everyone, no matter who they are, without causing pain to anyone?

It is not right to hurt someone and then only comfort those who deserve it. Some find it easy to bring comfort to those who are already at peace, but truly good people do not choose whom they help based on personal desires. Sometimes, even when a righteous person does not intend to cause harm, others may still feel troubled by their presence. This is often because the good person's actions reveal the flaws in others, making them uncomfortable.

Think of a man who owns a large estate filled with everything: children, servants, cattle, dogs, pigs, wheat, barley, hay, grass, and even acorns and meat. Because he is wise, he knows what to give each one. He gives bread to his children, simple food to his servants, barley and grass to the cattle, bones to the dogs, and acorns and slop to the pigs.

A true follower of God is like this man. He understands each person's soul and gives them what they need to grow. He does not judge people by their outward appearance but looks deeper into their spirit. To those who are like pigs, he gives what suits them. To those like cattle, he gives what they need. To those like children, he shares the fullness of divine wisdom.

There is the Son of Man, and there is the son of the Son of Man. The Lord is the Son of Man, and the son of the Son of Man is one who creates through the authority of the Son. The Son of Man was given the power to create and give life by God. Creating and giving life are two different things. A creator works in a way that everyone can see, while the one who gives life does so in a hidden way, unseen by the world. This hidden process is a deep mystery of divine unity.

Marriage in this world is a mystery, even to those who are part of it. No one truly knows the bond between a husband and wife except the two of them. If a physical marriage is already such a mystery, how much greater is the mystery of a spiritual marriage? This sacred union is pure, born from love, not physical desire. It belongs to the light, not the darkness. If a marriage becomes public, it loses its holiness and becomes ordinary. A bride should reveal herself only to those closest to her—her parents, the friend of the bridegroom, and the sons of the bridegroom. Others may only hear her voice or experience her presence from a distance, like dogs waiting for crumbs at their master's table.

When Abraham received a vision of what was to come, he circumcised himself as a sign of removing his earthly nature. In the same way, spiritual truths are hidden inside us, giving life, but if they are revealed too soon, they can bring harm instead.

As long as a tree's roots are hidden, it can grow strong. But if its roots are exposed, the tree will wither and die. The same is true for evil—when it remains hidden, it continues to grow in power. But once it is recognized and brought into the light, it disappears. This is why the Word says, "The axe is already at the root of the trees" (Matthew 3:10). The axe does not just cut the surface, because anything cut can grow back. Instead, it strikes deep, destroying evil at its source.

Jesus came to remove the root of evil completely, while others have only scratched the surface. We must also search within ourselves and remove any evil that remains. If we ignore it, it will continue to grow and control us, making us do things against our will. Ignorance is the source of all evil, keeping people trapped in sin and death.

Ignorance leads to death because those who live in ignorance have no foundation in truth. They never truly existed in the way that matters. They were, are, and will be nothing because ignorance produces nothing lasting. Truth, however, may seem hidden like ignorance at first, but when it is revealed, it brings life and is praised. As the Word says, "If you know the truth, the truth will set you free" (John 8:32). Ignorance enslaves, but knowledge brings freedom.

When we embrace the truth, we will see its fruits grow within us. By joining ourselves with truth, we are made whole, for knowing and accepting the truth is the key to freedom and eternal life. We must remove ignorance and cultivate truth, allowing it to transform us into beings of light and freedom.

Right now, we see the world as it appears on the surface. People are taught to admire the strong and powerful, while those who seem weak or unimportant are ignored. But in the divine realm, things are the opposite. What the world sees as weak is actually strong, and what is overlooked holds great value in the hidden truth. Though the mysteries of truth are revealed to us, they come in symbols and images, giving us only a glimpse of something far greater than we can fully understand.

The bridal chamber is the most sacred and profound of all mysteries. It is the most holy place, hidden from view. In the past, a veil covered the way God controlled creation, keeping divine truths secret. But when the veil was torn, those mysteries were revealed. When this world's time is over, it will no longer stand—it will be abandoned and eventually destroyed. The lesser powers that once ruled over it will flee, but they cannot enter the place of pure and perfect light, where the fullness of the divine exists. Instead, they will remain under the shadow of the cross, unable to reach the highest truth.

Those who are part of the divine priesthood will find safety when the flood of destruction comes. They will pass through the torn veil, just as the high priest once did, and enter the sacred space. The veil was not only torn from the top, which would have opened the way only for the heavens, nor from the bottom, which would have only revealed it to the earth. Instead, it was torn from top to bottom, opening a path from heaven to earth. The higher realms have revealed the mysteries of the lower realms so that we may understand divine truth.

This opening reveals a power and glory far greater than anything in this world. The perfection of the divine realm, along with its hidden mysteries, has now been made known to us. The holiest place has been revealed, and the bridal chamber welcomes those who wish to enter.

As long as evil remains hidden, it has no power. But it still exists among those who carry the Holy Spirit, controlling many people without them realizing it. When evil is exposed and brought into the light, the perfect light will shine over everything. Those who remain in this light will receive the anointing that sets them free. The enslaved will be freed, and those held captive will be released. As it is written, "Every plant my Father in heaven has not planted will be pulled up" (Matthew 15:13).

Those who were once separated from God will be reunited with Him and filled with His light. Everyone who enters the bridal chamber will carry this light, showing their eternal union with the divine. Unlike earthly marriages, which happen at night and fade away with the morning, the sacred marriage of the soul and the divine takes place in the light of day and lasts forever. This light never sets and never fades.

To become a child of the bridal chamber is to receive this eternal light. But if someone does not receive it in this life, they will not be able to receive it in the next. Those who receive the light of the bridal chamber become invisible to the powers of this world. They cannot be captured, harmed, or controlled, even while living in this world. And when they leave this world, they will already be filled with truth because they have encountered it through these mysteries.

For those who enter the bridal chamber, this world is transformed into something eternal, and they experience the divine realm in its fullness. To them, the truth is no longer hidden in darkness but is revealed in perfect light. This light never ends and shines on all who are united with it, guiding them toward the greatest mysteries of the divine.

The path to the bridal chamber is both an invitation and a discovery. It calls us to go beyond what we see in this world, to embrace the hidden truth, and to step into the eternal light where we are no longer held back by darkness and ignorance.

The Gospel of Judas

This is the secret message about judgment that Jesus shared with Judas Iscariot over eight days, three days before the Passover celebration.

When Jesus came to the world, he performed miracles to guide people toward salvation. Some chose to follow the right path, while others remained in their wrongdoing. This was how the twelve disciples were chosen. Jesus began teaching them about mysteries beyond this world and what would happen in the future.

Many times, he did not reveal everything about himself to his disciples. Sometimes, he even appeared among them as a child.

Jesus Criticizes the Disciples

One day, Jesus was with his disciples in Judea. He found them sitting together, deeply focused on their prayers. They had gathered in a circle, chanting solemnly as they prayed over the bread. When Jesus approached and saw what they were doing, he smiled softly.

Surprised, the disciples turned to him and asked, "Master, why are you smiling at our prayer? Have we done something wrong? Aren't we honoring God by doing this?"

Jesus looked at them and said, "I am not laughing at you. But you are not doing this because you truly desire it. You do it because you believe it will please your God."

Still confused, the disciples said, "Master, you are the Son of our God!"

Jesus looked at them thoughtfully and asked, "How do you truly know me? I tell you the truth—no generation of people among you will fully understand who I am."

Hearing this, the disciples became uneasy. Their confusion turned into frustration, and they felt anger rise in their hearts, upset by words they could not fully grasp.

But Jesus, knowing their thoughts and how they struggled to understand, spoke gently to them. "Why are you letting anger disturb your peace? Is it your God within you, or the stars that guide you, that have caused this unrest? If any one of you has the strength to bring forth true humanity, let that person stand before me now."

The disciples hesitated, glancing at each other. One by one, they claimed, "We are strong enough," but their doubt was clear, and none of them stood up.

Only Judas Iscariot found the courage to rise, but even he could not meet Jesus' eyes. Instead, he lowered his gaze, unable to face him directly.

Judas finally said, "I know who you are and where you came from. You come from the eternal realm of Barbelo. I am not even worthy to speak the name of the one who sent you."

Jesus, seeing that Judas spoke with sincerity, understood the thoughts stirring in his heart. He said to him, "Step away from the others, and I will share with you the mysteries of the kingdom. But know this: you will not enter the kingdom yourself. Instead, you will feel deep sorrow, because someone else will take your place to complete the twelve before their God."

Judas, troubled but eager to understand, asked, "When will you tell me these things? When will the great day of light come for the future generations?"

But Jesus, having spoken what he intended, withdrew from him and walked away.

Another Generation

The next morning, Jesus appeared again to his disciples. They were eager to ask him questions and said, "Master, where did you go? What were you doing when you suddenly left us?"

Jesus looked at them and said, "I went to another great and holy generation."

Confused, the disciples asked, "Lord, what generation could be greater and holier than us? Surely no such group exists anywhere else!"

When Jesus heard this, he smiled—not to mock them, but because he understood how limited their understanding was. He said, "Why are you struggling to understand the strong and holy generation I speak of? I tell you the truth—no one born into this world will ever see that generation. No army of angels from the heavens has power over it, and no human, bound by flesh, can enter it. The generation I speak of does not come from anything you know or from anything connected to this world."

He paused, giving them a moment to take in his words, then continued, "The generation I visited is not like the one here, which has been corrupted. The people among you belong to a world shaped by the powers and rulers of this earth, forces that control and govern everything you know. But the generation I speak of is beyond all of this. It is untouched, pure, and completely free from the influence of those born into this world."

As they listened, the disciples felt uneasy. His words seemed too vast, too mysterious for them to grasp. A deep silence fell over them.

They felt something powerful in what he said, but they could not yet understand its full meaning.

The Disciples' Vision

One day, Jesus came to his disciples, and they greeted him excitedly. They said, "Master, last night we had dreams about you, and what we saw was amazing!"

Jesus looked at them and asked, "Why are you hiding yourselves?"

They answered, "We saw a huge house with a beautiful altar inside. Around the altar stood twelve people—we think they were priests. There was a name written there, but we couldn't read it clearly. A large crowd was gathered in front of the altar, watching the priests perform rituals and accept offerings. We stood there too, trying to understand what was happening."

Jesus asked, "What did you see them doing?"

The disciples explained, "Some of the priests fasted for two weeks at a time. Others sacrificed their own children. Some left their wives behind and acted humble while singing praises. Others had relationships with men, committed murders, and did all kinds of sinful and criminal things. And Master, the people at the altar used your name while doing all of this! The priests filled the altar with blood and the remains of their sacrifices."

After telling him this, the disciples fell silent, disturbed by what they had seen.

Jesus, noticing their fear, said, "Why does this trouble you? I tell you the truth—those priests you saw at the altar are calling upon my name. But my name was written there by people, not by God. They have planted trees in my name, but those trees will never bear fruit."

He continued, "The altar and priests in your dream represent you. You are the ones standing before that altar. That altar belongs to the god you serve, and you are the twelve priests. The animals being sacrificed symbolize the people you mislead. Your leader will stand at that altar and use my name, and many devoted followers will trust in him. After him, another will lead those who give in to sin, another will support those who murder children, another will approve of men lying with men, and yet another will promote fasting, along with every kind of mistake, crime, and impurity.

"Some people say, 'We are equal to the angels,' but they are like falling stars, bringing destruction. It has been said, 'God accepts your sacrifice from the hands of priests.' But these priests serve a spirit of deception, not the Lord of all. On the last day, they will be judged for their actions."

Jesus then said, "Stop offering animal sacrifices on the altar. These sacrifices have already been given to the stars and angels you serve, but they mean nothing. Remove them from your midst so you can see the truth clearly."

The disciples, shaken by his words, pleaded, "Master, cleanse us from the sins we have committed because we were deceived."

Jesus answered, "It is not possible to erase all the mistakes of this generation. No single spring can put out the fire of the entire world, nor can one well provide water for all people. Only a great and steady source can do that. A single lamp cannot light up everything, except for the space it was meant to illuminate. In the same way, one baker cannot feed all of creation."

Hearing this, the disciples cried out, "Master, help us! Take this burden away from us!"

Jesus replied, "Stop resisting me. Each of you has your own star, and in the end, the stars will reclaim what belongs to them. I was not sent to this corrupt generation, but to the strong and incorruptible one. That generation has never been ruled by any enemy or controlled by the stars. Truly, I tell you, the pillar of fire will come quickly, and that incorruptible generation will not be shaken by the stars or anything else."

Jesus and Judas

When Jesus finished speaking to the group, he left, taking Judas Iscariot with him. As they walked, Jesus spoke to Judas in a calm but serious tone.

"The water that flows on the highest mountain does not come from the wells or rivers of this world," Jesus said. "It is not meant to feed the trees that grow corrupt fruit in this realm. Instead, it nourishes God's paradise, keeping the eternal fruit alive—fruit that never spoils. This water ensures that the path of life for the holy generation remains pure and everlasting."

Judas listened carefully, then asked, "Master, what kind of fruit does this generation produce?"

Jesus replied, "Every human soul will one day pass away. But when the chosen ones of this holy generation complete their time in the kingdom, their spirits will leave their earthly bodies behind. While their bodies will die like all others, their souls will live on forever, rising to the higher realms where they will exist eternally."

Still curious, Judas asked, "What about the rest of humanity? What will happen to everyone else?"

Jesus answered, "You cannot plant seeds on dry, rocky ground and expect a harvest. In the same way, the corrupted and mortal wisdom that created ordinary humans cannot bring them to the higher realms. Their souls will remain tied to this world. I tell you the truth—no ruler, no angel, and no power will ever see the place that this great and holy generation will inherit."

After saying this, Jesus stepped away. Judas stood there, deep in thought, then called out, "Master, as you have listened to the others, please listen to me now. I have seen a powerful vision."

Jesus turned back to him and chuckled softly. "Why are you so troubled, Judas, you thirteenth spirit? Speak, and I will listen."

Judas, unfazed by Jesus' words, continued, "In my vision, I saw myself surrounded by the twelve disciples. They were throwing stones at me and chasing me like an enemy. Then, I followed you to a place unlike anything I've ever seen. There was a house so enormous that I couldn't measure it with my eyes. Around it stood great and noble people, and the roof was covered in greenery. Inside, a large crowd had gathered, but I didn't understand why they were there. Master, please take me into this house and let me be among these people!"

Jesus looked at him and said, "Judas, your star has led you astray. No human born into this world can enter the house you saw—it is reserved for the holy and pure. In that place, there is no sun or moon, no day or night. Only those who are truly holy may live there, standing forever among the angels. I have already revealed to you the secrets of the kingdom and the errors of the stars. I have shown you what exists beyond the twelve realms you know."

With growing concern in his voice, Judas asked, "Master, my lineage doesn't rule over these realms, does it?"

Jesus replied, "Come closer, and I will tell you about the holy generation. But understand this—I am not telling you so that you may join them. Instead, you will feel great sorrow when you see the kingdom and its people, knowing that you cannot enter."

Judas, now filled with fear, asked, "Then what was the point of separating me from that generation?"

Jesus answered, "You will become the thirteenth, Judas. The other generations will curse you, and you will rule over them in their error. In the last days, people will turn to you in their confusion, but you will not rise to the holy generation, for it was never meant for you."

Jesus Reveals Everything to Judas

Jesus said, "Come closer, and I will reveal secrets no human has ever seen. There is a vast and endless realm, so great that even the angels cannot reach its boundaries. In this place lives a mighty and invisible Spirit, unseen by any angel, beyond human understanding, and without a name.

"A bright cloud appeared, and from it, the Spirit spoke, saying, 'Let an angel come into being to serve me.' From this cloud, a great angel was born—the Self-Begotten, the God of Light. Because of him, four more angels came from another cloud to serve him. The Self-Begotten then said, 'Let a new realm exist,' and so it was. He created the first great light to rule over it and called forth many angels to serve it.

"Then he said, 'Let another bright realm appear,' and it was created. He brought forth a second great light to rule there and assigned more angels to serve it. He repeated this process again and again, creating many realms of light, each with its own ruler and countless angels.

"In the first cloud of light was Adamas, a being no angel or divine figure could fully perceive. From Adamas came Seth, who was made in the image of the first great angel. From Seth, a pure and unbreakable generation was born. This generation brought forth twelve bright rulers, and these twelve created seventy-two more, as the Spirit willed. Each of the seventy-two produced five more, leading to a total of three hundred sixty rulers, each guiding a part of the twelve great realms.

"These twelve leaders shaped their own realms, each containing six heavens, adding up to seventy-two heavens in total. Each heaven had five firmaments, forming three hundred sixty firmaments. In each of these, there were countless armies of angels and pure spirits assigned to serve.

"This entire assembly is called 'the cosmos,' which the Father and the seventy-two rulers labeled as 'perishable.' Yet within it, the first human appeared, given unbreakable power. This realm also contained the cloud of wisdom and an angel called Eleleth. Eleleth said, 'Let twelve angels come forth to rule over Chaos and the underworld.' From this cloud appeared an angel with a fiery face, stained with blood. His name was Nebro, meaning 'Rebel,' though others called him Yaldabaoth. Another angel, Saklas, also emerged.

"Nebro created six angels to assist him, and Saklas did the same. Together, they brought forth twelve angels to rule the heavens, each given a share of power. These twelve rulers then decided to make humanity in their own image. Saklas said to his angels, 'Let us create a human being in our likeness.' So, they formed Adam and Eve, who, in the divine realm, is called 'Life,' because all generations seek him. Each generation knows her by a different name.

"Saklas, however, did not give them the ability to create life on their own. Instead, an angel spoke and declared that Adam's days, and those of his children, would be numbered."

Judas then asked Jesus, "Master, how long can a person live?"

Jesus answered, "Why does this surprise you? Adam and his descendants have limited lifespans because they belong to a kingdom ruled by Saklas."

Judas asked, "Does the human spirit die too?"

Jesus replied, "This is how it works: God told Michael to lend spirits to humans so they could live and serve. Later, the Great One ordered Gabriel to give spirits to the pure generation—spirits with souls. The rest of the souls, taken from the light but trapped in Chaos, search for the Spirit within them. It was God who gave Adam and his followers wisdom, so that the rulers of Chaos and the underworld would not have complete control over them."

Judas then asked, "What will happen to those future generations?"

Jesus said, "Listen carefully. The stars guide all things. When Saklas' time is complete, the first star of his generation will rise, and everything that was foretold will happen. These generations will sin in my name, committing terrible acts, harming children, and corrupting the world. They will offer these deeds to Saklas, who will rule over them. Then the twelve tribes of Israel will rise, and all generations will follow Saklas, continuing to sin in my name. And you, Judas, your star will rule over the thirteenth realm."

At this, Jesus laughed.

Judas, feeling uneasy, asked, "Master, why are you laughing at me?"

Jesus answered, "I am not laughing at you, Judas, but at the mistake of the stars. Six stars have fallen, along with five warriors, and what they have created will eventually be destroyed."

Judas then asked, "Master, what will happen to those who have been baptized in your name?"

The Betrayal

Jesus said, "Listen carefully—I tell you the truth, the baptism they have received in my name will bring about the downfall of this entire earthly generation. Tomorrow, they will bring suffering upon the one who carries my spirit. But know this: no human hand will ever truly take hold of me, and no earthly power will ever fully understand who I am.

"Judas, pay attention. Those who offer sacrifices to Saklas believe they are serving something greater, but in reality, they are only feeding the forces of evil. Yet, your actions will surpass all of them, for you will sacrifice the man who carries my spirit. Already, your strength has grown, your anger has been set ablaze, your star has risen, and your heart has strayed from its path.

"I tell you, the end is near. The rulers of this world are falling. The kings who once held power have become weak, and even the angels mourn their failure. The corruption they created is beginning to unravel, and their leader is approaching his destruction. When that moment comes, the chosen ones from the great generation of Adam will rise and be honored. They belong to the eternal realm, existing before heaven, earth, and even the angels were formed.

"Judas, look now—I have shared everything you need to know. Lift your eyes to the heavens and see. There is a radiant cloud of light, and within it, stars shine in a perfect circle. Among them, one star leads the way—that star is yours."

Judas, filled with wonder and fear, looked up and saw the brilliant cloud glowing above. The stars around it sparkled like a celestial choir. Drawn by an unseen force, Judas stepped forward and entered the cloud. As he rose into it, those left on the ground heard a voice echoing from within. Though the words were unclear, they spoke of a powerful generation and a destiny beyond human understanding.

Then, Judas was gone. He could no longer see Jesus, nor could anyone else.

Immediately, unrest spread among the Jewish leaders. The disturbance rippled through their ranks, and the high priests muttered among themselves in frustration. Jesus had gone into a guest room to pray, and they had failed to reach him. Watching closely from the shadows, the scribes waited for the right moment to act. Yet, they hesitated, afraid of the people, for many regarded Jesus as a prophet.

Then, Judas returned. The priests and scribes turned to him, their eyes filled with suspicion. They asked, "Why are you here? Aren't you one of Jesus' disciples?"

Judas hesitated for a moment, then spoke the words they had been hoping for. With his response, they found the confirmation they needed. Soon after, they handed him a sum of money in exchange for what he had done. In that moment, the plan they had been waiting for fell into place, and the events leading to Jesus' fate were set into motion.

The Authoritative Discourse

Chapter 1. Justin justifies his departure from Greek customs

Do not think, you Greeks, that my decision to separate myself from your traditions is foolish or thoughtless; I found nothing in them that is holy or pleasing to God. Even the works of your poets are just examples of madness and a lack of self-control. Anyone who learns from your most respected teachers ends up facing more problems than anyone else. For example, they tell how Agamemnon, to support his brother's excessive lust and madness, sacrificed his own daughter to make the gods happy. He even got all of Greece involved to get Helen back, who had been taken by a shepherd with leprosy.

Then, during the war, Agamemnon himself was controlled by his passion for Chryseis and started a fight with Achilles over Briseis. Achilles, your so-called hero who crossed rivers, destroyed Troy, and defeated Hector, was brought down by his love for Polyxena. He was even defeated by a dead Amazon warrior. He took off his armor, which was said to be made by the gods, and put on wedding clothes, becoming a sacrifice to love in Apollo's temple.

Ulysses from Ithaca turned bad behavior into something praised. His encounter with the Sirens showed he lacked real wisdom because he had to be physically tied down instead of using his own judgment to resist their temptation. Ajax, the son of Telamon, who carried a shield made of seven layers of oxhide, went mad when he lost the contest to Ulysses for Achilles' armor.

These are not the lessons I want to learn. This kind of so-called virtue is not something I want, and I cannot believe in the stories of Homer. The entire Iliad and Odyssey, from start to finish, focus on a woman, and I see no value in being taught such things.

Chapter 2. The Greek theogony exposed

After Homer, Hesiod wrote Works and Days, but who can take seriously the strange stories in his Theogony? They tell us that in the beginning, Chronos, the son of Ouranos, killed his father and took over his rule. Then, afraid that his own children might do the same to him, he began swallowing them. But with the help of the Curetes, Jupiter was secretly saved. Later, Jupiter trapped his father and divided the world into three parts: Jupiter took the sky, Neptune took the seas, and Pluto took the underworld.

Even with this division, things didn't go smoothly. Pluto kidnapped Proserpine, and Ceres searched desperately for her daughter. This story became central to the Eleusinian fire ceremonies. Neptune, meanwhile, harmed Melanippe while she was getting water and also attacked many Nereids. Listing them all would take too long.

As for Jupiter, he is known for his many affairs: he appeared as a satyr to Antiope, as a shower of gold to Danaë, and as a bull to Europa. To seduce Leda, he turned into a bird. His relationship with Semele showed both his unfaithfulness and Juno's jealousy. And then, he kidnapped the Phrygian boy Ganymede to be his cupbearer. These are the so-called great deeds of Saturn's sons.

And what about Apollo, the famous son of Latona, who claimed to have the power of prophecy? Even he was deceitful. He chased after Daphne but couldn't catch her, and though Hyacinthus loved him, Apollo didn't foresee the boy's tragic death.

I won't even get into Minerva's manly side, Bacchus's feminine traits, or Venus's wild desires. Instead, I suggest that the Greeks remind Jupiter of the laws against killing your father, the punishment for cheating, and the shame of his actions with Ganymede. Teach Minerva and Diana what women's duties are, and teach Bacchus what men should do. What's the point of a woman wearing armor or a man dressing up in women's clothes and leading a group of wild, drunken women?

Chapter 3. Follies of the Greek mythology

Hercules, famous in stories for his incredible strength and heroic deeds, is known as the son of Jupiter. He completed many impossible tasks, such as killing the mighty lion, defeating the many-headed hydra, and capturing the dangerous boar. He also brought down the fierce, man-eating birds, went to Hades to bring back the three-headed dog Cerberus, and cleaned the filthy Augean stables. Hercules fought fire-breathing bulls, killed a stag, picked golden apples from a guarded tree, and defeated the deadly serpent watching over them. He also defeated Achelous and Busiris for mysterious reasons and even crossed mountains to bring back magical water that could speak.

Despite all these amazing achievements, Hercules often acts in ways that seem childish. He got distracted by the noise of satyrs' cymbals, was swept away by a woman's love, and felt embarrassed when Lyda hit him. In the end, he died after putting on a poisoned tunic given to him by Nessus. Writhing in pain, he lit his own funeral pyre, ending his life in a tragic way.

And then there's Vulcan, the god who forges weapons. He's said to be envious of Mars because Mars is young and handsome, while Vulcan is old and deformed.

You Greeks, your stories show many flaws in your gods and heroes.

The gods often lack self-control, and your heroes are shown as weak and feminine. Look at the tales that shape your dramas: the curse on Atreus, the betrayal and scandal involving Thyestes, and the evil that plagued the house of Pelops. Danaus, filled with hatred, killed his relatives and left Ægyptus without any heirs. Then there's the gruesome Thyestean feast, which the Furies themselves prepared.

What about Procne, who is still said to fly in mourning, or her sister Philomela, who was silenced forever when her tongue was cut out? Do we need to mention Oedipus, who killed his father Laius, married his own mother, and had children who were both his sons and brothers, only for them to kill each other in a bitter feud? These stories form the core of your traditions, but they show a history full of violence, betrayal, and shame.

Chapter 4. Shameless practices of the Greeks

I can't stand your public gatherings. They are full of over-the-top feasts, the tempting music of flutes that stir up desire, wasteful oils for anointing, and garlands used for show and pride. These practices take away all sense of decency. Instead of focusing on building good character, you fill your minds with excess and give in to indulgence, making sinful behavior a normal part of life.

Let me ask you this: if you, as a Greek, get angry with your son for acting like Jupiter—rebelling against you or trying to seduce your wife—why do you still treat Jupiter as a god? How can you call your son an enemy for doing what Jupiter does, while you worship a god who acts in the same way? And why do you blame your wife for being unfaithful, yet honor Venus, the goddess who represents that very behavior?

If others made these accusations, you might brush them off as lies or slander. But your own poets celebrate these actions in their poems, and your history makes them known to all. These aren't just the opinions of critics; they are truths that your own traditions have passed down.

Chapter 5. Closing appeal

From now on, you Greeks, leave behind your old ways and embrace the wisdom that can't be matched. Learn from the Divine Word and come to know the immortal King. Don't idolize those who destroy nations through violence and war. Instead, recognize our Ruler, the Divine Word, who always helps us. He doesn't care about physical strength, outward beauty, or earthly pride. What He values is a soul made pure by holiness and led by good actions. The commands of our King aren't based on temporary power but on good deeds, because through the Word, true strength enters the soul.

Oh, the peace for the soul troubled by inner conflict! Oh, the power that defeats harmful desires! Oh, the teachings that put out the fire of sinful cravings! The influence of the Word is unlike anything you've known—it doesn't make poets, philosophers, or great speakers. Instead, by its guidance, it turns ordinary people into immortals and lifts them from the earth to higher places than even Olympus.

Come, be taught and transformed, for I was once like you. But I was changed—not by force, but by the power of the divine teachings and the strength of the Word. Just as a skilled healer drives a venomous snake from its home, the Word drives out the harmful desires of our nature from the deepest parts of our soul. It starts by removing lust, which is the root of all evils—hatred, anger, envy, and more.

When lust is gone, the soul becomes peaceful, calm, and free. No longer burdened by past sins, the soul is returned to its Creator. It goes back to the place it came from, the origin of every soul, and the place it's meant to return to.

The Apocalypse of Peter

Many people will claim to be prophets, but they will spread false teachings that lead others down the wrong path. These false teachers will bring destruction upon themselves.

Then God will come to those who remain faithful—those who long for righteousness, endure hardships, and keep their souls pure in this life. He will bring justice against those who live in wickedness.

The Lord then said, "Let's go up to the mountain and pray."

So we, the twelve disciples, followed him. We asked him to show us one of our righteous brothers who had passed away, so we could understand what they were like. We hoped this would give us courage and help us inspire others to believe in our message.

As we prayed, two men suddenly appeared before the Lord, facing the east. Their faces shone as brightly as the sun, and their clothes sparkled with a brilliance beyond anything we had ever seen. Their beauty and glory were indescribable, and we could barely look at them.

We stared in amazement. Their bodies were whiter than the purest snow, yet at the same time, they had a soft red glow, like the petals of the most vibrant rose. The red and white blended perfectly, making them look even more magnificent.

Their curly hair shimmered and flowed over their shoulders like a crown made of fragrant flowers. It reminded me of a rainbow stretching across the sky. Their presence was breathtaking.

They had appeared so suddenly that we were left in complete awe.

I turned to the Lord and asked, "Who are these men?"

He answered, "These are your righteous brothers, the ones you wanted to see."

Then I asked, "Where do all the righteous live? What kind of place is it that gives them such beauty and glory?"

The Lord then revealed a vast and radiant land beyond this world. It was brighter than anything I had ever imagined, filled with pure light, as if the sun itself shone from within it. The air glowed with warmth, and the ground was covered in flowers that never faded, releasing a sweet and refreshing fragrance.

This land was full of beautiful, everlasting plants and trees that produced the most blessed fruit. Even from a distance, the scent of this paradise reached us, filling the air with its heavenly aroma.

The people in this place wore clothes as bright and beautiful as the robes of angels, matching the incredible beauty around them. Angels floated above, making the place even more breathtaking. Everyone there shared the same glory, and they sang together with one voice, praising God with joy.

The Lord said to us, "This is where your high priests and the righteous live."

But then, I saw another place—dark, filthy, and terrifying. It was a place of punishment. The air was thick and heavy, as gloomy as the dark clothing worn by both the punishing angels and those being punished. Some people were hanging by their tongues—these were the ones who had spoken against the righteous path. Beneath them, fire burned, causing them constant pain.

A huge lake of flaming mud was filled with people who had used righteousness for their own selfish gain. Tormenting angels caused them endless suffering. Nearby, women hung by their hair over the bubbling mud. They had dressed themselves to lure others into adultery. The men who had sinned with them hung by their feet, their heads sinking into the filthy, boiling mire.

I thought to myself, "I never imagined such a terrible place could exist."

I saw murderers and their accomplices thrown into a cramped space filled with venomous snakes. The snakes bit them over and over, making them twist and writhe in pain. Dark, crawling worms covered them like a thick cloud, adding to their suffering. The souls of the people they had killed stood nearby, watching and saying, "O God, your judgment is fair."

Not far from there, I saw another tight space where blood and filth from the suffering people drained into a pool, forming a lake. Women sat in the filthy liquid, submerged up to their necks. Across from them sat the children they had conceived but aborted. The children cried out, and sparks of fire shot from their mouths, burning the women's eyes. These were the women who had caused abortions and were now cursed for their actions.

Elsewhere, men and women burned up to their waists in a dark place while evil spirits beat them. Worms ate them from the inside, never stopping. These were the ones who had betrayed and attacked the righteous.

Nearby, some men and women chewed on their own lips in torment while burning irons were pressed into their eyes. They had spoken against righteousness and spread lies. Others bit their own tongues, and fire shot from their mouths—these were the false witnesses.

In another part of this place, sharp, burning-hot stones, sharper than swords, covered the ground. Men and women dressed in torn, dirty clothes rolled on them, suffering without end. These were the rich people who had put their trust in wealth, ignored orphans and widows, and disobeyed God's commands.

In a huge, bubbling lake filled with blood and filth, people stood knee-deep in the disgusting mixture. These were the greedy lenders who charged others unfair amounts of interest.

Others were thrown off a high cliff. When they hit the ground, they were forced to climb back up, only to be thrown down again, never finding rest. These were the men who had dishonored their bodies by acting like women and the women who had lain with each other like a man and woman should.

Next to the cliff, fire burned where men who had made idols for themselves stood, trapped in the flames. Nearby, other men and women carried rods, striking each other over and over without end.

In another place, men and women burned and twisted in agony. Their bodies roasted in the flames. These were the ones who had abandoned God's way to chase after their own selfish desires.

The Revelation of Paul

Introduction

The Acts of Paul and Thecla is an old Christian story about Thecla, a devoted follower of the Apostle Paul. Written around the 2nd century, it focuses on faith, purity, and how God guides people's lives. These themes show the strong beliefs of early Christian communities.

Thecla's story is one of courage and deep faith. She defies society's expectations, survives persecution, and even performs miracles because of her strong belief in God. Her connection with Paul highlights the power of his teachings and how they helped spread Christianity.

Although this story is not included in the New Testament, it gives us a glimpse into the important role women played in early Christianity. It also shows how faith and preaching could transform lives. Thecla's story adds to our understanding of determination and faith, especially in difficult times.

The Acts of Paul And Thecla

A Christian writer named Tertullian said that this story was written by a church leader from Asia. When people questioned him, he admitted that he wrote it because he admired Paul. Later, Pope Gelasius officially declared that this story was not part of the Bible. However, many early Christians still believed it was true and accepted it as an important story. Well-known religious figures from the fourth century, including Cyprian, Eusebius, Epiphanius, Augustine, Gregory Nazianzen, Chrysostom, and Severus Sulpicius, all mentioned Thecla or talked about her story in their writings.

Basil of Seleucia wrote about Thecla's life, struggles, and victories in poetry. Around the year 590, a historian named Evagrius Scholasticus recorded a story about Emperor Zeno. After Zeno was forced to give up his throne to Basiliscus, he had a vision of Saint Thecla. In this vision, she told him he would get his throne back. When this actually happened, Zeno built a grand church in her honor in Seleucia, a city in Isauria, and gave it many gifts. According to Evagrius, these gifts were still being used even in his time.

Later, scholars such as Cardinal Baronius, Locrinus, Archbishop Wake, and Grabe (who edited the Septuagint and studied the Acts of Paul and Thecla) believed that these writings came from the time of the Apostles. They thought the story was free from superstition and fit well with Christian teachings of that time. Because of this, they saw it as an honest and trustworthy account.

Chapter. I.

When Paul escaped from Antioch and traveled to Iconium, two men named Demas and Hermogenes joined him. They acted like faithful followers, but in reality, they were not sincere.

Paul, who always focused on God's goodness, treated them with kindness and love. He patiently taught them about Christ, explaining the message of the Gospel and helping them understand God's revelation.

Meanwhile, a man named Onesiphorus heard that Paul had arrived in Iconium. Eager to meet him, he hurried to find Paul, bringing his wife, Lectra, and their two sons, Simmia and Zeno. They wanted to welcome Paul into their home. Even though they had never met him, Titus had described what Paul looked like, so they watched closely for someone matching that description.

They stood along the main road to Lystra, carefully observing every traveler. Eventually, they spotted Paul. He was a short man, bald, with slightly bent legs but well-shaped feet. His eyes were deep-set, and his nose was a bit hooked. His presence was graceful, and sometimes, his face seemed to glow like an angel's. Onesiphorus recognized him immediately and was filled with joy.

Onesiphorus warmly greeted Paul, saying, "Welcome, servant of the blessed God." Paul responded, "May God's grace be with you and your family."

However, Demas and Hermogenes, feeling jealous, acted as if they were true believers. Demas asked, "Aren't we also servants of God? Why didn't you greet us too?"

Onesiphorus replied, "I have not yet seen proof of righteousness in you. But if you show yourselves to be faithful, my home will be open to you as well."

Paul then entered the house of Onesiphorus, and the family was overjoyed. They prayed together, shared a meal, and listened as Paul preached about God's teachings. He spoke about the importance of living a pure life and the promise of resurrection. His sermon included these words:

- Blessed are those with pure hearts, for they will see God.
- Blessed are those who keep their bodies pure, for they will be God's temple.
- Blessed are those who practice self-control, for God will reveal Himself to them.
- Blessed are those who give up worldly pleasures, for they will be accepted by God.

- Blessed are those who are married but live with discipline, for they will be like God's angels.

- Blessed are those who respect God's word, for they will be comforted.

- Blessed are those who stay true to their baptism, for they will have peace with the Father, Son, and Holy Spirit.

- Blessed are those who follow the teachings of Jesus Christ, for they will be called children of the Most High.

- Blessed are those who obey Jesus Christ's instructions, for they will live in eternal light.

- Blessed are those who reject worldly fame for the sake of Christ, for they will sit beside Him and avoid final judgment.

- Blessed are those who remain pure in body and soul, for they are precious to God. Their faith will save them, and they will enjoy eternal rest.

Chapter. II.

As Paul preached in the house of Onesiphorus, a young woman named Thecla sat by the window of her own home, listening intently. Her mother, Theoclia, had arranged for her to marry a man named Thamyris, but Thecla was deeply moved by Paul's words.

Day and night, she stayed at the window, absorbing his teachings about God, faith in Christ, love, and prayer. She was so captivated that she wouldn't leave, listening with joy and growing more devoted to his message.

She watched as many women and young girls entered Onesiphorus's house to meet Paul. She longed to go too, to hear him speak up close, but she had only been able to listen from a distance.

As time passed, Thecla refused to eat or drink, completely focused on Paul's sermons. Worried, her mother called Thamyris, who arrived excitedly, expecting to see his future wife. He asked Theoclia, "Where is Thecla?"

Theoclia sighed and said, "Something strange has happened. For three days, Thecla has barely moved from the window. She hasn't eaten or drunk anything because she's so caught up in the words of a foreign man. I never imagined she would be so taken in."

She continued, "This man has stirred up the whole city of Iconium, and Thecla is just one of many. Young men and women are flocking to hear him speak. He teaches that there is only one God and that people should live pure and chaste lives."

Shaking her head, she added, "It's as if Thecla is trapped in a web, completely drawn in by his words. She listens eagerly, ignoring everything else. This has led her astray. Please, Thamyris, talk to her. She is supposed to be your wife."

Thamyris approached her carefully, not wanting to upset her. Gently, he said, "Thecla, my love, why are you sitting here like this? You look so distant and quiet. What has changed in you? Look at me, your betrothed, and speak to me."

Her mother pleaded too, saying, "My child, why won't you say anything? You seem lost in thought, as if you aren't even here. Please, speak."

But Thecla didn't react. She didn't look at them or acknowledge their words. Her mind was completely on Paul's teachings.

Thamyris grew desperate. He felt like he was losing her, and he wept. Theoclia cried for her daughter, and even the servants in the house joined in, mourning the change in Thecla.

But she remained unmoved.

Frustrated, Thamyris went into the streets, watching people come and go from Paul's gathering. While there, he saw two men arguing. He approached them and asked, "Who are you, and why are you here? Who is the man inside? I've heard he's leading people astray, convincing young men and women to abandon marriage."

Then he added, "I have power in this city. If you tell me the truth about him, I'll reward you."

The two men, Demas and Hermogenes, exchanged a look before answering. "We don't know much about him," they said, "but we do know this—he's persuading young men to leave their fiancées and telling women not to marry. He says there is no resurrection unless people stay pure and live without worldly attachments."

Chapter. III.

Thamyris then said, "Come to my home and enjoy a meal." So Demas and Hermogenes went with him to a grand feast, where the table was filled with rich food and plenty of wine.

As they ate, Thamyris encouraged them to drink freely, hoping to win their favor. His love for Thecla and his desire to marry her drove him to seek their advice.

During the meal, he asked, "Tell me, what exactly is Paul teaching? I am deeply worried about Thecla. She is so drawn to his words that I fear I will lose her."

Demas and Hermogenes, eager to turn Thamyris against Paul, answered, "If you want Thecla back, take Paul to Governor Castellius and accuse him of spreading Christian beliefs. The governor follows Caesar's orders, so he will have Paul executed. That will put an end to this nonsense, and you will have your bride again."

They added, "We will also explain to Thecla that the resurrection Paul talks about has already happened. It simply means bringing children into the world. We came alive again when we recognized God."

Thamyris was furious when he heard this.

The next morning, he gathered the city officials, the jailer, and a large crowd carrying sticks. Together, they marched to Onesiphorus's house. When they arrived, Thamyris confronted Paul and said, "You have caused trouble in Iconium. You have led many people astray, including Thecla, who was supposed to be my wife. Now she refuses to marry me. You must come with us to see Governor Castellius."

The crowd, growing angrier, shouted, "Get rid of this deceiver! He has misled our wives, and now everyone listens to him!"

Chapter. IV.

Paul accused before the governor by Thamyris. 5 Defends himself. 9 Is committed to Prison, 10 and visited by Thecla.

Thamyris stood before the governor and spoke loudly, saying, "Governor, I don't know where this man comes from, but he is teaching people that marriage is wrong. Order him to explain why he spreads these ideas."

As he spoke, Demas and Hermogenes leaned in and whispered to Thamyris, "Call him a Christian, and he will be sentenced to death immediately."

But the governor was careful. Turning to Paul, he asked, "Who are you? What exactly do you teach? These men are accusing you of serious things."

Paul responded with confidence, "Since I have been asked to explain my teachings, Governor, I ask that you listen to me.

"The God I serve is fair and perfect. He does not need anything from us, but He wants to save His people. He sent me to guide them away from evil, corruption, sinful desires, and death, and to lead them toward a life free from sin.

"For this reason, God sent His Son, Jesus Christ. I preach about Him and encourage people to put their hope in Him. Jesus showed incredible love and mercy to a lost world—not to condemn it, but to bring faith, respect for God, true worship, and a love for truth.

"So if all I am doing is teaching the truth that God has given me, what crime have I committed?"

After hearing this, the governor decided to have Paul arrested and kept in prison until he had more time to think about the case.

That night, Thecla took off her earrings and gave them to the prison guard. In return, he unlocked the doors and let her in.

She also gave a silver mirror to the jailer, who then allowed her to enter Paul's cell. Sitting at his feet, she listened as he spoke about God's power and goodness.

As she watched Paul, she saw that he was not afraid of suffering. His strength and courage came from his faith in God, and this inspired her even more. She was so moved that she kissed the chains that bound him.

Chapter. V.

Thecla sought and found by her relations. 4 Brought with Paul before the governor. 9 Ordered to be burnt, and Paul to be whipt. 15 Thecla miraculously saved.

Soon, Thecla's disappearance was discovered, and her family, along with Thamyris, searched the streets for her as if she had vanished. One of the porter's fellow servants informed them that she had left during the night.

They questioned the porter, who admitted that Thecla had gone to the prison to see the stranger. Following his directions, they rushed there and found her. After leaving the prison, they gathered a crowd and reported the situation to the governor.

Upon hearing this, the governor ordered that Paul be brought before him for judgment. Meanwhile, Thecla remained in the prison, lying on the floor where she had listened to Paul's teachings. When the governor summoned her as well, she eagerly accepted and went without hesitation.

As Paul was led forward, the crowd grew louder, shouting that he was a magician and demanding his execution. Despite their outrage, the governor paid close attention to Paul's teachings about the works of Christ. After speaking with his council, he turned to Thecla and asked, "Why do you refuse to marry Thamyris as the law of Iconium requires?"

Thecla remained silent, her eyes fixed on Paul. Seeing this, her mother, Theoclia, became furious and cried out, "Burn this wicked girl! Let her be burned in the theater for rejecting Thamyris, so that all women learn not to follow her example!"

The governor, troubled by the situation, ordered Paul to be whipped and expelled from the city. As for Thecla, he sentenced her to be burned at the stake. After giving his orders, he went straight to the theater, where a crowd had gathered to witness the execution.

As Thecla was led toward the stake, she looked around anxiously, like a lamb searching for its shepherd, hoping to see Paul. In the crowd, she spotted someone who looked like him and thought, "Paul has come to see me in my suffering." But as she gazed at him, he disappeared into the sky before her eyes.

Young men and women carried wood and straw to build the fire. As Thecla approached the stake, the governor was struck by her beauty, and tears filled his eyes. The crowd told her to step onto the wood, and she obeyed, making the sign of the cross before doing so.

The fire was set, and though the flames rose high, they did not harm her. God showed mercy and caused the ground beneath to shake while dark clouds above released heavy rain and hail. The earth's tremors put many in danger, and some even lost their lives. The fire was extinguished, and Thecla was saved.

Chapter. VI.

Paul with Onesiphorus in a cave. 7 Thecla discovers Paul; 12 proffers to follow him: 13 he exhorts her not for fear of fornication.

Paul, along with Onesiphorus, his wife, and their children, was fasting in a cave on the road from Iconium to Daphne. They had gone without food for several days when the children said, "Father, we're hungry, and we don't have any money to buy bread." Onesiphorus had given up everything to follow Paul with his family.

Paul removed his coat and handed it to the boy, saying, "Take this and go buy some bread."

While the boy was out getting food, he spotted Thecla, his neighbor, and was surprised to see her. "Thecla, where are you going?" he asked.

She replied, "I'm looking for Paul. I was saved from the fire."

The boy said, "Come with me! Paul has been very worried about you. He's been praying and fasting for six days."

When Thecla arrived at the cave, she found Paul kneeling in prayer.

He was saying, "Holy Father, Lord Jesus Christ, please protect Thecla from harm. Help her, for she is your servant."

Standing behind him, Thecla called out, "Lord, Creator of heaven and earth, Father of your beloved Son, I thank you for saving me from the fire and allowing me to find Paul again."

Paul stood up, and when he saw her, he said, "God, who knows all hearts, Father of my Lord Jesus Christ, I thank you for hearing my prayer."

Everyone in the cave—Paul, Onesiphorus, and the others—was filled with joy. They shared five loaves of bread, some herbs, and water, comforting each other by reflecting on Christ's teachings.

Then Thecla said to Paul, "If you allow me, I will follow you wherever you go."

Paul replied, "People are quick to fall into sin, and since you are beautiful, I fear you might face even greater temptations than before. You may struggle to resist them."

Thecla answered, "Give me the seal of Christ, and no temptation will overcome me."

Paul responded, "Be patient, Thecla, and in time, you will receive Christ's gift."

Chapter. VII.

Paul and Thecla go to Antioch. 2 Alexander, a magistrate, falls in love with Thecla: kisses her by force: 5 she resists him: 6 is carried before the governor, and condemned to be thrown to wild beasts.

Paul sent Onesiphorus and his family back home while he continued on to Antioch, bringing Thecla with him.

When they arrived, a respected Syrian official named Alexander noticed Thecla and immediately became infatuated with her. Wanting to gain Paul's favor, he offered him expensive gifts.

But Paul refused, saying, "I don't know the woman you're talking about, and she doesn't belong to me."

Still determined, Alexander, who was a powerful man in Antioch, grabbed Thecla in the street and kissed her. Feeling deeply disturbed, Thecla searched for Paul and cried out in distress, "Don't touch me! I am a servant of God and a stranger here. I am a noblewoman from Iconium, and I left my city because I refused to marry Thamyris."

She then grabbed Alexander, ripped his coat, pulled the crown from his head, and made a scene in front of everyone, humiliating him.

Though embarrassed, Alexander still felt drawn to her. But his anger and wounded pride won over his desire, and he dragged her before the governor.

When Thecla admitted to what she had done, the governor ruled that she would be thrown to the wild beasts.

Chapter. VIII.

Thecla entertained by Trifina; 3 brought out to the wild beasts; a shelion licks her feet. 5 Trifina upon a vision of her deceased daughter, adopts Thecla, 11 who is taken to the amphitheatre again.

When the people saw what was happening, they began to speak out, saying that the city's judgments were unfair. Meanwhile, Thecla made a request to the governor, asking for her purity to be protected until the time came for her to face the wild beasts.

The governor asked if anyone would take her in, and a wealthy widow named Trifina, who had recently lost her daughter, stepped forward. She offered to care for Thecla and welcomed her into her home, treating her like her own child.

When the day arrived for the beasts to be released, Thecla was taken to the amphitheater. She was placed in a den with a fierce lioness while a large crowd gathered to watch. Trifina stayed by Thecla's side without fear. To everyone's shock, the lioness didn't attack Thecla but instead licked her feet. Above her, a sign was placed that read "Sacrilege," marking the crime she had supposedly committed. Many women in the audience cried out, saying the city's judgments were cruel and unjust.

After the beasts were displayed, Trifina took Thecla back to her home. That night, as she slept, Trifina had a vision of her deceased daughter, Falconilla. In the vision, Falconilla said, "Mother, let Thecla take my place as your daughter. Ask her to pray for me so that I may find eternal happiness."

Deeply moved, Trifina woke up in sorrow and told Thecla about the vision. "My daughter appeared to me and asked me to accept you as my own. Please, Thecla, pray for her so that she may be granted eternal joy and life."

Hearing this, Thecla immediately knelt down and prayed, "O Lord, God of heaven and earth, Jesus Christ, Son of the Most High, please allow Falconilla to live forever in your presence."

Trifina, still overcome with grief, cried out, "How cruel these judgments are! How can the world be so unjust that such a pure soul as Thecla must once again face the beasts?"

The next morning, at dawn, Alexander arrived at Trifina's house and demanded, "The governor and the people are waiting. Bring out the prisoner now." But Trifina, filled with anger and sorrow, confronted him so fiercely that he became frightened and fled.

A woman of royal lineage, Trifina cried out, "I am drowning in grief! I have already lost my daughter, and now I can do nothing to save Thecla. O Lord, help your servant in her time of need."

As Trifina prayed, the governor sent an officer to retrieve Thecla. Holding her hand, Trifina said, "I walked with Falconilla to her grave, and now I must walk with you, Thecla, to face the beasts."

Hearing these words, Thecla was moved to tears. As they walked, she prayed, "O Lord, my refuge and strength, bless Trifina for her kindness and for protecting me. Show her your love."

When they reached the amphitheater, chaos erupted. The beasts roared, and the crowd shouted for Thecla to be brought in. The tension in the arena grew as voices rose in protest.

Some people yelled, "Let the whole city suffer for these crimes! Governor, punish us all the same way. This is unjust and cruel!"

Others cried out, "Destroy the city for this wickedness! Kill us all, Governor. This is a terrible injustice!"

Chapter. IX.

Thecla thrown naked to the wild beasts; 2 they all refuse to attack her; 8 throws herself into a pit of water. 10 other wild beasts refuse her. 11 Tied to wild bulls. 13 Miraculously saved. 15 Released. 24 Entertained by Trifina.

Thecla was taken from Trifina's care, stripped of her clothing, dressed in a simple belt, and thrown into the arena where wild beasts were waiting. Lions and bears were released to attack her. A fierce lioness approached her, but instead of attacking, it lay down at her feet.

The women in the audience gasped and shouted in amazement.

Next, a bear charged toward Thecla, but the lioness jumped in and killed it. Then a large lion, owned by Alexander and known for attacking men, rushed at her. The lioness fought fiercely to protect Thecla, and after a brutal struggle, both animals died. The crowd, especially the women, were heartbroken to see the lioness that had defended Thecla lose its life.

More wild animals were released, but Thecla stood her ground with her hands raised to the sky in prayer. When she finished praying, she noticed a pool of water nearby. She said, "Now is the perfect moment for me to be baptized." She jumped into the water and declared, "In your name, Lord Jesus Christ, I am baptized on this final day."

The crowd, including the governor, panicked and yelled for her to stop, fearing that deadly sea creatures in the water would attack her. But Thecla didn't hesitate. She threw herself into the water in the name of Jesus Christ.

As she entered, lightning struck the water, and flames appeared, killing the sea creatures. Their bodies floated to the surface while a glowing fire surrounded Thecla, protecting her and covering her nakedness from the crowd. More wild animals were set upon her, but the spectators began throwing fragrant spices, perfumes, and oils into the arena. The air filled with the strong scent, and the animals became drowsy, lying still instead of attacking Thecla.

Alexander, determined to see her killed, suggested to the governor that they use bulls to finish the job. The governor hesitated but finally agreed, saying, "Do as you wish."

Thecla was tied to two strong bulls, and red-hot irons were pressed against them to make them run wildly and drag her across the arena. The bulls roared and struggled, but suddenly, the fire surrounding

Thecla burned through the ropes, setting her free. She stood in the arena unharmed, as if she had never been bound at all.

Watching from her seat, Trifina fainted and appeared lifeless. The crowd erupted in chaos. Seeing this, Alexander, now terrified, turned to the governor and begged, "Please, have mercy on me and the city. Release this woman who has survived everything, or we will all be doomed. If Caesar hears of what happened and learns that Trifina, a woman of royal blood and related to him, has died here, he will punish the entire city."

The governor called Thecla forward and asked, "Who are you, and why haven't the beasts harmed you?"

Thecla answered, "I am a servant of the living God. I believe in Jesus Christ, His Son, who is pleasing to God. That is why the beasts could not touch me. He is the only way to eternal life. He is the refuge for the troubled, the strength for those in pain, and the hope for the hopeless. Anyone who does not believe in Him will face eternal death."

The governor, moved by her words, ordered that her clothes be brought to her and said, "Put on your clothes."

Thecla replied, "May the God who clothed me among the beasts clothe your soul with salvation on the day of judgment." She dressed herself, and the governor immediately announced, "I release Thecla, the servant of God."

The women in the crowd shouted in praise, declaring, "There is only one God—the God of Thecla, who has saved her!" Their voices were so loud that it felt as if the whole city shook.

At that moment, Trifina woke up, alive and well, and ran to Thecla. Hugging her tightly, she said, "Now I believe in the resurrection of the dead. Now I know my daughter lives. Come home with me, Thecla, and I will give you everything I have."

Thecla stayed with Trifina for a few days, teaching her about the Lord. Many young women were inspired by her story and converted to the faith, bringing great joy to Trifina's household.

However, Thecla longed to see Paul again. She searched everywhere until she learned that he was in Myra, in Lycia. Determined to find him, she gathered a group of young men and women, dressed as a man, tied a belt around her waist, and set out for Myra.

When she arrived, she spotted Paul among the crowd, preaching the word of God. Without hesitation, she walked up and stood beside him.

Chapter. X.

Thecla visits Paul. 8 Visits Onesiphorus. 8 Visits her mother. 9 Who repulses her. 12 Is tempted by the devil. Works miracles.

Paul was shocked when he saw Thecla and the people with her. He thought they might be facing another challenge. Sensing his concern, Thecla reassured him, saying, "Paul, I have been baptized. The same God who helps you in your preaching also helped me baptize myself."

Paul then took Thecla to the house of Hermes. There, she told him everything that had happened to her in Antioch. Paul was amazed, and everyone who heard her story grew stronger in their faith. They also prayed for Trifina's well-being.

After some time, Thecla stood up and said, "I am going back to Iconium." Paul replied, "Go and share the word of the Lord." Before she left, Trifina sent Paul a large sum of money and clothing through Thecla to help the poor.

When Thecla arrived in Iconium, she went to the house of

Onesiphorus. She fell to the ground where Paul had once sat and preached. With tears in her eyes, she mixed her prayers with her sorrow, saying, "O Lord, the God of this house, where I first came to know You; O Jesus, Son of the living God, who saved me from the governor, the fire, and the wild beasts; You alone are God forever and ever. Amen."

Upon her return, Thecla found that Thamyris had died, but her mother, Theoclia, was still alive. She approached her and said, "Mother, can you believe that there is only one true God who lives in heaven? If you desire great riches, God will provide them through me. If you wish to have your daughter back, here I am."

Thecla spoke to her mother at length, trying to convince her to believe in Christ, but Theoclia refused to accept her words. Realizing that her efforts were in vain, Thecla made the sign of the cross over herself and left her mother's house.

She then traveled to Daphne and returned to the cave where she had first met Paul and Onesiphorus. There, she fell to the ground and wept before God.

From there, she journeyed to Seleucia, where she taught many people about Christ. A bright cloud guided her throughout her travels. When she arrived, she stayed just outside the city, about a furlong away. She remained cautious of the locals, as they worshipped idols.

The cloud led her to a mountain called Calamon, or Rodeon, where she stayed for many years. During this time, she faced strong temptations from the devil but overcame them with the help of Christ.

Over time, noblewomen heard about Thecla's devotion and traveled to learn from her. Many of them left their former lives behind and joined her in living a monastic life.

Her reputation spread far and wide. She performed many miraculous healings, and people from the city and nearby regions brought their sick to her. Even before reaching the entrance of her cave, the sick were healed. Evil spirits were cast out with loud cries. Everyone who came to her was healed and praised God for giving such power to Thecla.

Because of her miracles, the doctors in Seleucia lost many of their patients and their income. Filled with jealousy, they began to plot against Thecla, the servant of Christ.

Chapter. XI.

Is attempted to be ravished, 12 escapes by a rock opening, 17 and closing miraculously.

The doctors, filled with jealousy, let evil thoughts take over their minds. One day, as they gathered to discuss their plans, they said to each other, "The virgin Thecla is a priestess of the great goddess Diana. Everything she asks for is granted because she is pure, and all the gods favor her. We must find a way to ruin her."

They came up with a plan to hire a group of reckless young men. After getting them drunk and offering them a large sum of money, they instructed them to go and defile Thecla, promising an even greater reward if they succeeded. They believed that if these men corrupted her, the gods would no longer favor her, and Diana would stop granting healing through her.

Following their plan, the men climbed the mountain and approached her cave like wild animals. They banged on the door, determined to carry out their wicked mission.

Thecla, trusting fully in God, opened the door. She already knew their intentions but remained calm. Looking at them, she asked, "Young men, why have you come here?"

They replied, "Is there a woman named Thecla here?"

She answered, "What do you want with her?"

They said, "We want to be with her."

Thecla responded firmly, "I am just a humble servant of my Lord Jesus Christ. Though you have evil intentions, you will not succeed."

They laughed and said, "We will do whatever we want to you. Nothing can stop us."

As they reached out to grab her, she remained calm and spoke gently, "Young men, wait and witness the power of the Lord."

She lifted her eyes to heaven and prayed, "O God, You are greater than all. You have defeated Your enemies. You saved me from the fire, from Thamyris, and from Alexander. You protected me from wild beasts and deep waters. You have always helped me and shown Your glory through me.

"Now, Lord, save me from these wicked men. Do not let them destroy the purity I have kept for You. I love You, long for You, and worship You, O Father, Son, and Holy Spirit, forever. Amen."

Suddenly, a voice from heaven said, "Do not be afraid, Thecla, my faithful servant. I am with you. Look at the place I have prepared for you. It will be your eternal home, where you will see the glory of God."

Thecla looked beside her and saw the rock open wide, just large enough for her to enter. Trusting the voice, she escaped into the rock. As soon as she was safely inside, the rock closed behind her, leaving no trace of an opening.

The men stood in shock, unable to stop her or do her any harm.

The only thing they managed to grab was a piece of her veil, which tore as she escaped. This happened by God's will so that those who visited the sacred site in the future would have proof of her story and believe in Jesus with pure hearts.

And so, Thecla's trials came to an end. She was the first martyr and apostle of God, a virgin fully devoted to His service. She had left Iconium at eighteen years old and spent her life traveling and living in her cave in devotion. She lived to be ninety before the Lord took her to heaven.

Her life came to an end, and her memory is honored on the twenty-fourth of September, giving glory to the Father, the Son, and the Holy Spirit, now and forever. Amen.

The Revelation of James

Chapter 1

James, a servant of God and the Lord Jesus Christ, writes to the twelve tribes scattered around the world: Greetings to you.

My brothers and sisters, find joy even when you face struggles and hardships. Remember, when your faith is tested, it builds patience and endurance. Let patience do its full work in you so that you may grow and become complete, lacking nothing.

If you need wisdom, ask God. He gives generously to everyone without criticism, and He will give it to you. But when you ask, believe without doubting. Someone who doubts is like an ocean wave tossed around by the wind. Such a person should not expect to receive anything from the Lord because they are divided in their thinking and unstable in all they do.

Let those who are humble take pride in being lifted up by God, and let the rich take pride in being humbled. Riches are like flowers in a field—they bloom for a while but soon fade away. The sun rises with scorching heat, and the flowers dry up, fall, and lose their beauty. In the same way, the wealthy will disappear while chasing their own goals.

Blessed is the one who stays strong during trials. After passing the test, they will receive the crown of life that the Lord has promised to those who love Him.

When you are tempted, do not say, "God is tempting me." God cannot be tempted by evil, and He does not tempt anyone. Instead, each person is tempted when they are drawn away by their own desires.

These desires give birth to sin, and when sin is fully grown, it leads to death.

My dear brothers and sisters, do not be fooled. Every good and perfect gift comes from above, from the Father of lights, who never changes like shifting shadows. By His own will, He gave us new life through the word of truth so that we would be like the first fruits of His creation.

So, my dear brothers and sisters, be quick to listen, slow to speak, and slow to get angry. Human anger does not produce the righteousness that God desires.

Get rid of all moral filth and evil, and humbly accept the word that has been planted in you—it has the power to save your soul.

Do not just listen to the word and deceive yourselves—do what it says. Someone who hears the word but does not act on it is like a person who looks in a mirror, sees their reflection, and then walks away, immediately forgetting what they look like. But the one who looks carefully into the perfect law that gives freedom and continues in it—not just hearing but acting on it—will be blessed in what they do.

If someone thinks they are religious but does not control their words, they are fooling themselves, and their religion is meaningless.

True and pure religion that pleases God the Father is this: caring for orphans and widows in their struggles and keeping yourself from being corrupted by the world.

Chapter 2

My dear brothers and sisters, do not claim to follow our glorious Lord Jesus Christ while treating some people better than others. Imagine a man wearing fancy clothes and a gold ring comes to your gathering, and a poor man dressed in worn-out clothes also arrives. If you give special attention to the rich man, saying, "Sit here in a good seat," but tell the poor man, "Stand over there" or "Sit on the floor by my feet," aren't you making unfair judgments based on appearances?

Listen, my beloved brothers and sisters: Didn't God choose the poor of this world to be rich in faith and heirs of His kingdom, which He promised to those who love Him? But you have treated the poor with disrespect. Isn't it the rich who take advantage of you and drag you into court? Aren't they the ones who insult the honorable name by which you are called?

If you truly follow the royal law in Scripture—"Love your neighbor as yourself"—then you are doing what is right. But if you treat people unfairly, you are sinning and will be judged by the law as a wrongdoer. If someone obeys the entire law but breaks just one part, they are guilty of breaking all of it. The same God who said, "Do not commit adultery," also said, "Do not murder." So if you avoid adultery but commit murder, you are still a lawbreaker.

Speak and act as those who will be judged by the law that gives freedom. God will show no mercy to those who have not been merciful. But mercy is greater than judgment.

What good is it, my brothers and sisters, if someone claims to have faith but does nothing to show it? Can that kind of faith save them? Suppose a brother or sister has no clothes and nothing to eat, and one of you says, "Go in peace, stay warm, and have plenty to eat," but does nothing to help—what good is that? In the same way, faith by itself, without action, is useless.

Someone might say, "You have faith, and I have deeds." But I will show you my faith by what I do. You believe in one God—good! But even demons believe that, and they tremble in fear.

You foolish person, do you need proof that faith without action is worthless? Think about Abraham, our ancestor. Wasn't he considered righteous for what he did when he placed his son Isaac on the altar? His faith and his actions worked together, and his faith was made complete by what he did. This fulfilled the Scripture that says, "Abraham believed God, and it was credited to him as righteousness." That is why he was called God's friend.

You see, a person is made right with God through their actions, not just by faith alone. In the same way, Rahab, the prostitute, was considered righteous because she welcomed the spies and helped them escape safely.

Just as a body without a spirit is dead, faith without action is also dead.

Chapter 3

My dear brothers and sisters, not many of you should want to become teachers, because teachers will be judged more strictly. Teaching is a big responsibility, and we all make mistakes in different ways. If someone can completely control their words and never say the wrong thing, they are truly mature and able to control their whole body as well.

Think about how we put bits in a horse's mouth to guide it—such a small tool can direct the whole animal. The same is true for ships. Even though they are large and pushed by strong winds, a tiny rudder steers them wherever the pilot wants them to go. In the same way, the tongue is small but has the power to say great things. Just like a tiny spark can start a huge fire, our words can cause enormous harm.

The tongue is like a fire, spreading evil and corruption. It can ruin a person's entire life, and its destructive power comes from the forces of hell itself. People have learned to tame every kind of animal—wild beasts, birds, reptiles, and sea creatures—but no one can completely tame the tongue. It is restless, full of evil, and as dangerous as deadly poison.

With our tongues, we praise the Lord, our Father, but we also use the same tongue to curse people—people who were made in God's image. This should not happen! A spring cannot give both fresh and bitter water. A fig tree cannot grow olives, and a grapevine cannot grow figs. In the same way, a saltwater spring cannot produce fresh water.

Who among you is truly wise and understanding? Let them prove it by living a good life, showing humility and wisdom through their actions. But if you are filled with jealousy and selfish ambition, do not pretend otherwise or twist the truth. These attitudes do not come from God; they come from the world, from human desires, and even from evil forces. Wherever there is jealousy and selfishness, there will also be chaos and all kinds of wrongdoing.

But the wisdom that comes from God is different. It is pure, peaceful, kind, and willing to listen to others. It is full of mercy and produces good things. It is fair and completely honest. Those who work for peace will plant seeds of goodness, and in return, they will harvest a life filled with righteousness. Peaceful actions lead to a life of goodness, and those who create harmony will enjoy the blessings of the Lord.

Chapter 4

Why do you have conflicts and arguments with each other? Don't they come from the selfish desires inside you? You want things but can't have them. You are jealous, even willing to hurt others, but still don't get what you want. You fight and argue, but you don't have what you need because you don't ask God. And even when you do ask, you don't receive because your reasons are selfish—you only want things for your own pleasure.

You unfaithful people, don't you realize that being too attached to this world makes you an enemy of God? Whoever chooses to follow the ways of the world turns against God. Do you think the Scriptures mean nothing when they say that the spirit God gave us has a strong tendency toward jealousy? But God gives even greater grace. That is why it says, "God stands against the proud but gives grace to the humble."

So give yourselves fully to God. Resist the devil, and he will run away from you. Come closer to God, and He will come closer to you. Wash your hands, sinners, and make your hearts pure, you who are divided in loyalty. Feel the weight of your sins—be truly sorry and repent. Turn your laughter into sadness and your joy into sorrow. Humble yourselves before the Lord, and He will lift you up.

Do not speak badly about one another, my brothers and sisters. If you judge or criticize a fellow believer, you are judging God's law instead of following it. And if you judge the law, you are no longer living under it but acting as if you are above it. There is only one true Lawgiver and Judge—the One who has the power to save or destroy. So who are you to judge your neighbor?

Listen, those of you who say, "Today or tomorrow we will go to a certain city, do business there for a year, and make money." You don't even know what will happen tomorrow! What is your life? You are like a mist that appears for a short time and then disappears. Instead, you should say, "If it is the Lord's will, we will live and do this or that." But instead, you boast about your own plans, and such boasting is wrong.

So if you know the right thing to do but choose not to do it, you are sinning.

Chapter 5

Listen, you who are rich—weep and mourn for the troubles that are coming your way. Your wealth is rotting away, and your fancy clothes are full of holes from moths. Your gold and silver are rusting, and that rust will be proof against you. It will destroy you like fire because you have selfishly stored up wealth in these last days.

Look! The wages you refused to pay the workers who harvested your fields are crying out against you. The Lord of Heaven's Armies has heard the cries of those who worked for you. You have lived in luxury, satisfying your every desire without care. You have made yourselves fat, like animals being prepared for slaughter. You have condemned and killed innocent people who could not fight back.

So, my brothers and sisters, be patient as you wait for the Lord to return. Think about a farmer who waits for his crops to grow, trusting the early and late rains to come. You must also be patient and keep your hearts strong because the Lord's coming is near. Do not complain about each other, or you will be judged. Look—the Judge is standing at the door!

Think about the prophets who spoke in the Lord's name. They suffered, but they remained patient. We consider those who endured through hardships to be blessed. You have heard about Job's faithfulness and how, in the end, the Lord took care of him. The Lord is kind and full of mercy.

Above all, my brothers and sisters, do not swear by heaven, earth, or anything else. Instead, let your "yes" mean yes and your "no" mean no, so that you will not be judged.

If anyone among you is suffering, they should pray. If someone is happy, they should sing songs of praise. If anyone is sick, they should call the elders of the church to pray over them and anoint them with oil in the name of the Lord. The prayer made in faith will heal the sick, and the Lord will raise them up. If they have sinned, they will be forgiven.

So confess your sins to each other and pray for one another so you may be healed. The prayer of a righteous person is powerful and effective.

Elijah was a person just like us. He prayed earnestly that it would not rain, and for three and a half years, no rain fell on the land. Then he prayed again, and the sky poured down rain, making the earth produce crops once more.

My brothers and sisters, if one of you strays from the truth and someone helps bring them back, remember this: Whoever helps a sinner turn from their wrong path saves them from death and covers a multitude of sins.

The Revelation of Adam

The Testament of Our Father Adam

Introduction

The Testament of Adam is an ancient text that is said to have been written by Adam, the first man in the Bible. It has been preserved in different languages and gives a mystical and prophetic view of the universe, worship, and the future redemption of humanity. This text provides insight into early Jewish and Christian beliefs, combining religious ideas with visions of the end times.

The text focuses on three main ideas: the sacred hours of the day and night, Adam's prophecy about the coming of the Messiah, and a vision of the world's future. The first part explains how each hour of the day and night is dedicated to praising God—by angels, animals, heavenly beings, and even nature itself. This idea shows the harmony of creation and how God's presence is everywhere.

The second part contains a prophecy in which Adam predicts the coming of Christ. After being cast out of Paradise, Adam receives a promise from God that His Word will become human, be born from a virgin, and perform miracles to save people. This vision closely matches Christian beliefs about Jesus, making the Testament of Adam important for understanding early Christian ideas about the Messiah.

The final section describes the destruction and renewal of the world. Adam speaks of a great flood that will cleanse the earth because of the evil of Cain's descendants and also predicts that, in the end, the world will be purified by fire. These ideas are similar to themes found in biblical and other ancient texts about the end times.

Beyond its religious meaning, the Testament of Adam is part of a larger tradition of Jewish and Christian mystical writings, where history, divine messages, and the order of the universe are connected. It encourages readers to think about the patterns of worship and God's promises for the future. Whether seen as a prayerful text, an apocalyptic message, or an early Christian testimony, the Testament of Adam offers a deep reflection on humanity's role in God's plan.

By discussing the sacred hours, the prophecy of Christ, and the future of the world, this text connects the ancient past with the distant future. It serves as a reminder of the hope of salvation and the power of God over all things.

The Hours of The Day.

Understand this about the hours of the day and night, and how important it is to pray to God at the right times. My Creator taught me these things. He showed me the names of all the animals, the birds in the sky, and how each hour has a special meaning. He also revealed to me how the angels give praise to God.

Listen, my child, and know this:

- At the first hour of the day, my children's prayers rise up to God.
- At the second hour, the angels lift their prayers and requests to Him.
- At the third hour, the birds in the sky sing His praises.
- At the fourth hour, the spiritual beings worship Him.
- At the fifth hour, all the animals and wild creatures honor Him.
- At the sixth hour, the Cherubim make their petitions to Him.

- At the seventh hour, all the angels come before God and then leave His presence. At this time, every living thing's prayer reaches Him.
- At the eighth hour, the bright heavenly beings praise Him.
- At the ninth hour, the angels who stand before God's throne give Him honor.
- At the tenth hour, the Holy Spirit touches the waters, making the evil spirits flee. If the Holy Spirit did not bless the waters at this time each day, no one would be able to drink from them because evil spirits would make the water harmful. But if a priest takes water at this hour, mixes it with holy oil, and anoints the sick or those troubled by evil spirits, they will be healed.
- At the eleventh hour, the righteous people give their praises to God.
- At the twelfth hour, God listens to the prayers and requests of all people.

The Hours of The Night.

- At the first hour of the night, even the demons give thanks and praise to God Most High. During this time, they do not cause harm or trouble until they finish their worship.
- At the second hour, the fish and all sea creatures, including the great whales, lift their praises to God.
- At the third hour, fire itself gives praise. During this time, the fire is in the deepest parts of the earth, and no one can speak to God.
- At the fourth hour, the Seraphim (heavenly beings) declare God's holiness.

- At the fifth hour, the waters above the heavens give praise. Long ago, I listened to the angels at this hour and was amazed by the sound of their voices. They cried out like a powerful wheel turning, and their voices roared like ocean waves as they praised God.

- At the sixth hour, the clouds praise God with fear and trembling.

- At the seventh hour, everything on earth becomes still. The land and all creatures grow silent, and even the waters rest. If a priest takes water at this time, mixes it with holy oil, and anoints the sick or those struggling to sleep, the sick will be healed, and the restless will find sleep.

- At the eighth hour, the earth brings forth grass, plants, and trees, causing them to grow leaves and fruit.

- At the ninth hour, the angels continue their worship, and the prayers of people rise up to God Most High.

- At the tenth hour, the gates of heaven open, and God listens to the prayers of believers. He answers the requests of those who call upon Him. At this moment, when the Seraphim spread their wings, the roosters crow and praise God.

- At the eleventh hour, joy spreads across the earth as the sun enters Paradise. Its light reaches all corners of the world, shining on everything that exists.

- At the twelfth hour, my children should stand before God and honor Him. At this time, a great silence falls over the heavens as all creation shows reverence.

Adam Foretells the Coming of Christ.

Now, listen carefully and understand this: The Word of God, the Most High, will come down to earth just as He told me when He sent me out of the Garden of Paradise. He said that in the future, His Word would become human, born from a virgin named Mary. He would take on flesh and be born as a man with great power, wisdom, and skill. Only He and those to whom He chooses to reveal Himself will truly know Him.

God told me that He would walk among people, grow older over the years, and perform many miracles. He would walk on water as if it were solid ground, command the sea and the wind, and they would obey Him. He would heal the blind, cleanse those with leprosy, make the deaf hear, and allow the mute to speak. He would heal those who were paralyzed, help the lame walk, lead many people away from false beliefs to the knowledge of God, and cast out demons from those who were possessed.

God also spoke to me and said, "Do not be sad, Adam. You wanted to become like a god and broke my command. I will restore you, but not now—it will happen in time." Then He said, "I am God, and I sent you out from the Garden of Joy into this world, where the ground will grow thorns and weeds. You will live here, your back will bend with age, your knees will grow weak, and your body will return to the earth to be eaten by worms. But after five and a half days, I will have mercy on you. I will come into your home, take on human flesh, and be born as a child. I will live among people, walk in the marketplace, fast for forty days, be baptized, suffer, and die on the cross—all of this I will do for you, Adam."

May He be praised, honored, and glorified forever and ever, along with His Father and the Holy Spirit. Amen.

And know this, my son Seth: A great flood will come and wash over the whole earth because of the wickedness of Cain's children. Cain, the murderer, killed his brother out of jealousy over their sister, Lud. After the flood, many years will pass, and the last days will come. Everything will be completed, and the time of judgment will arrive. Fire will consume everything before God, and the earth will be made holy again. Then, the Lord of Lords will walk upon it.

Seth wrote down this message and sealed it with his own seal, along with the seals of his father, Adam, and his mother, Eve—seals that had been taken from the Garden of Paradise.

Thank You for Reading

Dear Reader,

We hope this timeless classic has sparked your imagination and enriched your literary journey. Now that you've turned the final page, we want to share a vision for the future of reading—one where every classic you've ever wanted to explore is at your fingertips, in a format that best suits your life.

We'd like to invite you to gain immediate, unlimited digital & audiobook access to hundreds of the most treasured literary classics ever written—along with the option to secure deluxe paperback, hardcover & box set editions at printing cost. Together, we can spark a new global literary renaissance alongside our small, independent publishing house called "The Library of Alexandria."

Thousands of years ago, the Library of Alexandria stood as a beacon of knowledge—until it was lost to history. We aim to reignite that spirit of preservation and discovery right now, in the modern age—only this time, it's accessible to all, in every language and every format.

Picture a world where every timeless classic, novel, poem, or philosophical treatise is not only available to read but also updated for today's readers—modernized, translated into any language or dialect, and ready to enjoy in any format you choose, whether that is in an eBook, audiobook, paperback, or deluxe hardcover & box set version a printing cost.

By joining our movement to rebuild the modern Library of Alexandria, you become part of an unprecedented mission to offer:

- **Unlimited Audiobook & eBook Access to the Greatest Classics of All Time**

  Instantly explore thousands of legendary works, from Plato and Shakespeare to Jane Austen and Leo Tolstoy. All are instantly ready to read or listen to, giving you a complete literary universe at your fingertips.

- **Paperback & Deluxe Editions at Printing Costs:**

  Purchase any title in a paperback, deluxe hardbound, or deluxe boxset edition at printing costs, shipped right to your doorstep. Curate your personal library of Alexandria with editions worthy of display—crafted to last, designed to captivate, and delivered straight to your door.

- **Modern translations for Contemporary Readers in all languages and dialects**

  Discover a vast selection of classics reimagined in clear, current language—no more struggling with outdated phrases or obscure references. Next to the original versions, we aim to offer translations in as many languages and dialects as possible.

  As we continue our translation efforts and add new languages, readers everywhere can connect with these works as if they were written today. By bridging linguistic divides, you're contributing to ensuring that these timeless stories become more meaningful, accessible, and inspiring for people across the globe.

- **Your Personal Library of Alexandria:**

  Over the months and years, you'll curate a unique physical archive of classics—each volume a testament to your taste, curiosity, and love of knowledge. It's not just about owning books—it's about curating a cultural legacy you'll cherish and pass down for generations to come.

- **Join a Global Literary Renaissance:**

  Your support fuels an ongoing mission: allowing us to reinvest in offering deluxe print editions (including special boxsets) at their true cost, broaden the range of available formats and translations, and extend the reach of these works to new audiences worldwide. By joining today, you're not just preserving a legacy of masterpieces; you set in motion a powerful wave of literary accessibility.

  We are more than a publisher—we're a movement, and we can't do it alone. Your support lets us scale our mission, preserving and reimagining history's greatest works for tomorrow's readers.

Become a Torchbearer of knowledge.

Thank you for picking up this book and allowing us into your literary journey. As you turn the pages, know that you're part of something larger: a global effort to keep these stories alive, share their wisdom across borders and generations, and spark a true cultural revival for the modern era.

If this resonates with you—please consider taking the next step by visiting:

www.libraryofalexandria.com

With gratitude and a shared love of knowledge,

The Modern Library of Alexandria Team

Visit:

www.libraryofalexandria.com

Or scan the code below:

www.ingramcontent.com/pod-product-compliance
Lightning Source LLC
LaVergne TN
LVHW030633080426
835509LV00022B/3462